# Leadership and Generalship in the Civil War

# LEADERSHIP AND GENERALSHIP
## IN THE
# CIVIL WAR

*Edited by* John W. Knapp

Virginia Sesquicentennial of the American Civil War Commission
Richmond, Virginia

©2013 by the
Virginia Sesquicentennial of
the American Civil War Commission

All rights reserved. First edition, published 2013.
Printed in the United States of America on acid-free paper.

ISBN 978-0-9834012-2-3

The fourth in a series of seven Signature Conferences sponsored by the
Virginia Sesquicentennial of the American Civil War Commission,
"Leadership and Generalship in the Civil War" was held
March 22, 2012 at the Center for Leadership and Ethics
at the Virginia Military Institute.

Library of Congress Control Number: 2012948646

Virginia Sesquicentennial of the American Civil War Commission
Richmond, Virginia

www.VirginiaCivilWar.org

## Contents

Preface · vii

### Panel I: Supreme Command: Lincoln and Davis

The Military Genius of Abraham Lincoln Revisited · 1
*Mark E. Neely*

Jefferson Davis as War Leader · 15
*William J. Cooper*

### Panel II: Lee and the Army of Northern Virginia

Lee and His Detractors in the Age of the Anti-Hero · 27
*Robert K. Krick*

Robert E. Lee and the Three Obligations of Command · 41
*Carol Reardon*

### Panel III: Grant and the Army of the Potomac

What Was Grant Like? · 53
*Josiah Bunting*

Grant on the Eve of the Wilderness Campaign · 63
*James I. Robertson, Jr.*

## Panel IV: The Valley Campaigns, 1862 and 1864

The 1862 Shenandoah Valley Campaign: Abraham Lincoln and the Union Defeat  
*Peter Cozzens* — 77

The 1864 Shenandoah Valley Campaign: Military and Political Significance  
*Jeffry D. Wert* — 85

## Concluding Address

The Importance of Studying Military History  
*Gary Gallagher* — 97

Appendix: Leaders and Generals of the Civil War — 111

Appendix: Further Reading — 127

Contributors — 133

Index — 137

# Preface

On March 22, 2012, the fourth annual Signature Conference, sponsored by the Virginia Sesquicentennial of the American Civil War Commission, convened at the Virginia Military Institute in Lexington, Virginia. Nine distinguished historians and scholars presented papers to a full house in Marshall Hall at the Center for Leadership and Ethics. The subject of the conference was Leadership and Generalship in the Civil War. The Civil War has been described as the most traumatic episode in the history of our Republic, and its legacy includes powerful examples of the successes and failures of its leaders, both political and military, which deserve renewed and continued study by all Americans.

The war in Virginia was the principal focus of the conference, and understandably so, since more than half of the major land battles were fought in Virginia. The land conflict was framed by the first battle at Manassas, Virginia, in 1861, and by the end-of-war engagement at Appomattox, Virginia, in 1865. Concomitantly, the state suffered a greater share of bloodshed and ruin than any other state.

This conference had special meaning for the Institute. Not only did more than nine out of ten of the approximately 2000 men who had attended VMI (between its founding in 1839 and the advent of war) see active service during the war, but the Corps of Cadets was called out fifteen times in various support roles; the most notable was the Battle of New Market in May 1864, when the cadets' heroic charge turned the tide of battle, which resulted in the loss of ten lives and 47 wounded. Retribution came in June 1864, when invading Union forces shelled and burned the Institute. Today, at the edge of the VMI Parade Ground you can see the graves of six of the ten who died at New Market. Further, you can find in the City of Lexington the burial sites of Confederate Generals Robert E. Lee and Stonewall Jackson as well as the wartime Governor of Virginia, John Letcher.

Early in the planning process for the conference, VMI Superintendent General J. H. Binford Peay III set a goal for the program committee: to offer an understanding of the challenges of leadership during that most difficult time in our nation's history. In a subsequent conversation, Civil War historian James M. McPherson suggested that an overarching theme of the conference might be "the principles of effective command." With that in mind, the program committee focused deliberation on the following lines:

*Supreme Command.* In a constitutional democracy, how does the president—given political realities—define war aims, mobilize and sustain the populace, and select generals-in-chief? How did Lincoln and Davis meet these demands?

*Officers and Soldiers.* What was the background and experience of the officers selected to build, train, and lead the armies? How were leaders developed during the war? How do we assess the hosts they led? How did Lee and Grant meet these tests?

*Leadership Traits.* What are the enduring qualities of successful generals? What caused success and failure—events or personalities or both?

*Legacies.* What lessons in leadership and in the art and craft of war came out of the Civil War? How did they affect wars of the last century and a half? How will military studies impart these legacies to future generations?

The papers reproduced in this volume attest that the conference agenda and presentations successfully accomplished our purposes. One will find here the propositions that the success of backwoodsman Abraham Lincoln as a war leader was "the product of genius not of growth," and that Jefferson Davis, while richly prepared and successful in many areas, was perhaps not ruthless

Virginia Military Institute Barracks, damaged in Hunters Raid of June 1864. Lexington, Virginia, 1866. VMI Archives.

enough "to make absolutely essential command decisions." Here, too, one will find penetrating analyses of Robert E. Lee's ennobled presence and genius and of Ulysses S. Grant's far-reaching strategic growth and selfless service during the war, after decidedly lackluster pre-war experiences.

In the sessions on the Valley Campaigns of 1862 and 1864, which were included to highlight independent command, one finds intriguing arguments that failures in 1862 at the higher levels of Federal command were a large factor in the brilliant success attributed to Stonewall Jackson; however, in 1864 a reversal in Federal command relationships promoted Philip Sheridan's success.

In a concluding address on the importance of studying military history, Gary Gallagher makes the compelling case that military events are central to understanding the political and social dimensions of a conflict like the Civil War and, by implication, any other war. There is the added reward in military history of encountering "a feast of dramatic incidents, memorable characters, and striking contrasts of skill and ineptitude, of gallantry and perfidy, of triumph and shattering defeat." When we resolve to remember those who gave their lives in the Civil War, Gallagher goes on, it is because they fought nobly as citizen-soldiers representing all of us. They are the source of the very meaning of the war and its sacrifices.

I have enjoyed the privilege of holding the Floyd D. Gottwald, Jr. '43 Visiting Professorship in Leadership and Ethics at Virginia Military Institute. My principal charge has been to prepare for and then to chair this Signature Conference. It could not have been accomplished without the support and assistance of the individuals and offices included in the acknowledgements section that follows. As a Superintendent Emeritus and Professor Emeritus of the Institute, I have been handsomely rewarded by a recall to duty and participation in the Leadership and Ethics program at the Institute which is now a formal part of the core curriculum. A thorough understanding of leadership and ethics has always been an imprint of a VMI education, and it is encouraging to see these subjects explored in programs like this 2012 Signature Conference.

## Acknowledgments

In their welcoming remarks, General Peay and Speaker William J. Howell noted the strong mutual support between the host institution, Virginia Military Institute, and the sponsoring agency, the Virginia Sesquicentennial of the American Civil War Commission, in producing this Signature Conference. As the head of their respective organizations, each of these leaders provided a clear sense of direction and unwavering dedication to bringing forth a first-rate conference.

Foremost among those who deserve recognition for this conference, the fourth in a series of seven from 2009 through 2015, is the able and indefatigable Executive Director of the Commission, Cheryl Jackson. She, more than anyone else, deserves credit for having met the Commonwealth's aims of commemorating the 150th anniversary of the war.

Also deserving of recognition and high praise for the publication of these proceedings is Kathleen DuVall, Communications Coordinator for the Commission staff. She is the person mainly responsible for ensuring coherence and readability of the conference papers, for adherence to a single style sheet, and for producing the final page proofs. Her consummate professional skills have been invaluable in the process. The Commission's history intern Amanda Kleintop goes on to graduate school this year, but not before having contributed in important ways to this volume as she did to those that came before it.

Other members of the Commission staff who contributed to the success of the conference include Michele Howell, Scott Maddrea, Barbara Teague, and Chris McCormick, who organized and assisted with registration, hospitality, and transportation functions. Not to be overlooked is Maggie Jackson, who served as volunteer assistant as she has done at all the conferences.

At the VMI conference site, planning, staging, and other local arrangements were coordinated by the Center for Leadership and Ethics in Marshall Hall. The Director of the Center, Captain Susan J. Rabern, USN (Retired), is the highly capable leader of a staff that includes: Amy DeHart, Robert Deyo, Derek Pinkham, Justin Spears, Margaret Weimer, and Kathy Wirtanen. They are an experienced and effective team, and the conference was hugely successful largely because of their keen hands-on efforts.

As conference chairman, I was fortunate to be guided and assisted over a period of two and one half years by a program committee consisting of Brigadier General Charles F. Brower IV, Professor of International Studies at VMI; Dr. J. Holt Merchant, Professor of History at Washington & Lee University; and Colonel A. Cash Koeniger, Professor of History at VMI (these three having served with me as panel moderators during the conference). Also serving at various times on the program committee were Colonel Malcolm Muir (now retired) and Colonel Kenneth E. Koons, both Professors of History at VMI, and Colonel Keith E. Gibson, Executive Director of VMI Museum Operations.

Other VMI personnel who provided valuable assistance were Colonel Rob McDonald, Associate Dean of the Faculty; Patricia Leahy, Office Manager in the Dean's Office; Michael A. Lynn, Site Director of the Stonewall Jackson House (under VMI Museum Operations); and Chief Michael L. Marshall the VMI Police.

Many persons and institutions outside of VMI contributed to the planning and execution of the conference and supported local events before and after. The Virginia Horse Center, whose Executive Director is Katherine Truitt, granted the use of their parking facilities as the off-site terminal for the conference busing operations. At Washington & Lee University, Linda Donald, Manager of Lee Chapel, assisted with visitations there; and Clover Archer Lyle, Director of Staniar Gallery in the Lenfest Center, worked with Colonel Rob McDonald to offer an art exhibit lasting several weeks.

Finally, I must give special thanks to Jean Clark, Director of Tourism for Lexington and Rockbridge County. She also serves as chair of the local Lexington/Rockbridge Sesquicentennial Committee, an allied function with the Virginia Commission activities in Richmond. From the very beginning of our conference planning efforts, Jean and her committee members gave us valued advice and support.

*John W. Knapp*
*Lieutenant General (VA)*
*Conference Chair*

# Leadership and Generalship in the Civil War

# The Military Genius of Abraham Lincoln Revisited

Mark E. Neely, Jr.

No presidential campaign in American history hinged more on military history than did the election of 1864, which pitted the commander-in-chief against his one-time general-in-chief. We do not often think of the election of 1864 in such terms, but they were true of the contest between President Abraham Lincoln, running for re-election, and General George B. McClellan, his Democratic opponent.

At issue between them were not the usual partisan platform planks—disagreements over tariff rates or interpretations of the Fugitive Slave Law. The main issue turned out to be the military record of General McClellan and the abilities of the president as commander-in-chief. It is safe to say that the most divisive issue in the election of 1864 was the utility of strategy itself. Nowhere else in the Civil War do we find better proof of historian Gary Gallagher's assertion, found elsewhere in this volume, that the study of military history is essential for understanding almost all facets of the American Civil War.

The divisive military issue was simple: McClellan's failure in the Peninsula Campaign of 1862. Did McClellan lose all by himself because he was too cautious and slow, or did Lincoln cause him to lose by withholding for the defense of Washington tens of thousands of men that McClellan needed to win his battles in Virginia?

Because of the political circumstances of the presidential campaign of 1864, General McClellan's official report, *The*

Abraham Lincoln campaigning for U.S. Senate. Chicago, Illinois, 1854. Photographer Polycarp von Schneidau. Library of Congress Prints and Photographs Division.

*Organization of the Army of the Potomac, and of Its Campaigns in Virginia and Maryland,* became a political campaign document. It underwent a scrutiny that no similar official military report had ever endured before. Widely reviewed in the press, McClellan's book elicited mostly unthinkingly partisan criticism and praise. However, one anonymous reviewer, at least, managed to offer moderate and thoughtful consideration of the report.

The review appeared in the *Round Table,* a pro-Democratic

magazine briefly published in New York City during the war. In answering the all-important question, "Was [McClellan] or the administration more to blame for the failure of the Peninsular campaign?" the anonymous reviewer criticized Lincoln's performance as commander-in-chief this way:

> It is hardly just . . . to judge the Administration too severely. Mr. Lincoln honestly wished to do what was best, but partly on account of his circumstances and partly because of his education he could not act very differently from what he did. The training of a lawyer is not very well fitted for making a good general. A planner of campaigns needs breadth of view, comprehensiveness, directness, a knowledge of how to make time his ally; but the legal mind while active loses in breadth what it gains in sharpness and intensity. Mr. Lincoln could not understand why, if a rebel army could be whipped at the West, it was not done at once, overlooking all the remote consequences. To "move on the enemy's works" was all that was required to gain victories. It is somewhat remarkable that, of the large numbers of lawyers who have entered the armies, North and South, so few have achieved real distinction.

This passage raises questions about the influence of Lincoln's legal training on his ideas of military strategy. Did his ideas on strategy and war, faulty or not, come from events as early in life as the ones that shaped his views on the Constitution?

In his youth, before he ever set foot in a courtroom, Lincoln developed his understanding of the Constitution from three main influences—nationalism, the Whig party platform, and the antislavery movement.

Lincoln grew up on the frontier, but the time was at least as important as the place; he grew up in the aftermath of the War of 1812. Born in 1809, he was six years old when that disastrous war ended in 1815. Intelligent Americans realized that the U.S. essentially lost the war. They realized as well that defeat stemmed from want of resources and unity. It seemed clear that one did not really have a country if there were no roads on which to move troops. Likewise, there was no country where there were no banks and no means to pay troops and few manufactured goods with which to arm troops. So the end of the War of 1812 ushered in what historians often call the age of nationalism in the U.S. The young Lincoln imbibed from the spirit of the times the results of a massive campaign to make America a nation. A sincere nationalism would be crucial to his anti-secessionist understanding of the Constitution.

The second source of Lincoln's constitutional ideas was the economic development platform of the Whig party. For Lincoln, these views were at first existential and less a matter of political partisanship. As a poor boy who grew up on hardscrabble farms owned by his illiterate father, Lincoln hated the frontier because of its lack of genuine economic opportunity. How was a poor but ambitious boy to escape from a hard life of subsistence agriculture? Without roads, or canals, or other transportation, how could he ever leave the farm? How could he get ahead without banks to offer loans? Farmers could not get surplus products to market or borrow money to improve and expand production, and Lincoln could not escape the frontier.

The Whig party held the answer in a program of government subsidized economic development: internal improvements (or what we call infrastructure), protective tariffs to develop manufacturing, and a national bank to pool capital for loans and to supply stable currency for financial transactions. Of course, the Constitution does not say in so many words that the government can build canals and roads or establish banks. To be a Whig was to have a broad outlook on the powers of Congress to encourage economic development. So Lincoln became a broad constructionist.

The third source for Lincoln's understanding of the Constitution was the antislavery movement. The Constitution was a problem for the antislavery movement, because it clearly sanctioned slavery. Slavery was mentioned three times in the document: in the three-fifths compromise on representation, in the provision to delay outlawing the international slave trade, and in the notorious fugitive slave clause. The antislavery movement's solution to this terrible problem was to maintain that the Constitution never refers to slavery by name—only by some euphemism like "people held to service or labor." Such circumlocutions, they argued, were proof that the Founding Fathers were ashamed of slavery and looked forward to its eventual demise. Lincoln took the argument to heart and thus saw the Constitution as an essentially liberal document.

These three sources of Lincoln's constitutional ideas originated in his youth. Surely this was also true of his ideas on command and strategy. The clever reviewer in the *Round Table* was wrong: nothing really important to Lincoln's outlook came from his legal training or practice of law, not even his ideas on the Constitution.

A quick survey of books on Lincoln as commander-in-chief reveals that they generally begin in 1861 and examine what he learned once the Civil War began. Historians tend to play down and make light of Lincoln's previous military experience, three months' service in the Black Hawk War when he was 23 years old. This is because Lincoln himself made light of it in a very funny speech in Congress in 1848, often called the "military coattails" speech. During the military campaign in the Black Hawk War, he never saw a hostile Indian or fired a shot, apparently. In the speech given over 15 years later in which he recalled his experience as an Indian fighter, Lincoln made fun of presidential aspirants (such as the Democrat Lewis Cass, in particular) whose claims to military heroism seemed laughable.

Congressman Lincoln then spoke of his own military experience at the greatest length he ever allowed to the subject:

> By the way, Mr. Speaker, did you know I am a military hero? Yes sir; in the days of the Black Hawk war, I fought, bled, and came away. Speaking of Gen. Cass's career, reminds me of my own. . . . I guess I surpassed him in charges upon the wild onions. If he saw any live, fighting Indians, it was more than I did; but I had a good many bloody struggles with the musquetoes.

Lincoln already knew how to manipulate the stories of his past to fit a political situation, and it would be a mistake to imagine that his time on military campaign was laughable. It was not.

The testimony of other veterans of the Black Hawk War reveals that Lincoln, if he did not see any "live, fighting Indians," nevertheless must have got an eyeful of war. One of Lincoln's fellow volunteers in that war in his New Salem days was a man named Royal Clary, and he described what Lincoln must have seen on that campaign but did not himself describe:

> The Indians . . . had killed Davis & Pettigrews family—Halls two girls with them; they were young women. We saw the scalps

they had taken—scalps of old women and children. . . . The Indians scalped an old grandmother . . . hung her scalp on a ram rod—that it might be seen and aggravate the whites—They cut one woman open—hung a child that they had murdered in the woman's belly that they had gutted—strong men wept at this—hard hearted men cried.

Lincoln and the other volunteers had seen plenty to provoke them, but another of Lincoln's comrades in arms, William Greene, in an oral history interview given just after Lincoln's death, recalled:

An old Indian came to camp and delivered himself up, showing us an old paper written by Lewis Cass, stating that the Indian was a good and true man. Many of the men of the Army said "we have come out to fight the Indians and by God we intend to do so." Mr. Lincoln . . . got between the Indian and the outraged men—saying—"Men this must not be—he must not be shot and killed by us."

This revealing anecdote, told by more than one witness, demonstrates that there was a special quality to the leadership abilities Lincoln showed early. If Lincoln began to establish his aura of leadership in the Black Hawk War, as seen in his election to captain, the quality of that leadership by the time his service terminated was already distinguished by an appeal to "the better angels of our nature."

It would be a mistake to ignore such experiences, even if Lincoln himself did not point us in their direction. It is a mistake, too, to think such memorable events had no bearing on his career as commander-in-chief. His experience in the Black Hawk War offered clear indications that one set of the most important military ideas President Lincoln held was already firmly in place when Lincoln was a youthful militiaman: An inclination to protect noncombatants from indiscriminate slaughter and thus to exercise moral restraint in war.

This inclination developed early in Lincoln's life and persisted ever after. One of Lincoln's most important ideas as commander-in-chief was to distinguish always between combatant and noncombatant and to prevent or restrain atrocity. He articulated this idea in August 1863 while defending the Emancipation

Proclamation:

> Armies, the world over, destroy enemies' property when they can not use it; and even destroy their own to keep it from the enemy. Civilized belligerents do all in their power to help themselves, or hurt the enemy, except a few things regarded as barbarous or cruel. Among the exceptions are the massacre of vanquished foes, and non-combatants, male and female.

The commonest modern historical narrative pattern for the Civil War assumes a gradual breakdown of the laws of war in the course of the conflict. It assumes that atrocities increased, gruesome guerrilla warfare grew endemic, and the enemy's people became targets as much as the armies. Some of this occurred, no doubt, but President Lincoln was sure to resist it rather than encourage it. The lesson of "total war" on some 20th-century model, if it presented itself to be learned from the developments of the Civil War, was wasted on Lincoln, who maintained the restraints customary in European conflicts.

There is no denying that Lincoln learned some important grand-strategic ideas while he was president and commander-in-chief. But we do not know the source of even the most important of these ideas. Perhaps the most important of all was a simple idea that can be described anachronistically as understanding the nature of war before the germ theory of disease. President Lincoln understood it by December 1862. The only source is secondhand. It comes from a conversation Lincoln had in the White House with his private secretaries, recorded by one of them, William O. Stoddard, just after the Union's disastrous defeat at Fredericksburg:

> We lost fifty per cent more men than did the enemy, and yet there is sense in the awful arithmetic propounded by Mr. Lincoln. He says that if the same battle were to be fought over again, every day, through a week of days, with the same relative results, the army under Lee would be wiped out to its last man, the Army of the Potomac would still be a mighty host, the war would be over, the Confederacy gone, and peace would be won at a smaller cost of life than it will be if the week of lost battles must be dragged out through yet another year of camps and marches, and of deaths in hospitals rather than upon the field. No general yet found can face the arithmetic, but the end of the war will be at hand when he shall be discovered.

The fatality statistics from the Crimean War and the American Civil War were available for all to see, but how many strategists really noticed that twice as many died in camp as from enemy action? Lincoln was interested in those statistics and understood that the awful arithmetic of such warfare dictated a strategy of having no strategy, of engaging in combat with the enemy as often as possible to get the business over with. The source of this idea in Lincoln is uncertain, but among Civil War leaders, only Lincoln understood it so clearly.

Lincoln's broad conception of the necessity for action rather than sickly inaction bore some relation to his overall suspicion of strategy and maneuver, which proved to be the great sticking point between the commander-in-chief and his general-in-chief, George B. McClellan. Lincoln's differences with McClellan arose so quickly after the initial Bull Run disaster in July 1861 that we can be sure that Lincoln had a predisposition to prefer advance. After all, both the president and the general could read anywhere in the newspapers apologies from journalists who were sorry they had pressed an unready army to the Bull Run defeat. After the battle many had second thoughts about having pressed the Union "on to Richmond" before it was really organized and prepared. McClellan learned from the experience, and indeed, seemed to have learned all too well, organizing, preparing, disciplining, and planning in defiance of public opinion and renewed Northern impatience. Lincoln wanted the army better prepared, too, but he put the lesson behind him quickly.

Where did Lincoln's persistently urgent desire for military advance come from? It seems all but certain that Lincoln's early life accounts better for his impatience with strategy than his growth in office and learning on the job. One of the early sources of constitutional attitudes was important also in this realm of military thinking: Lincoln's struggle with poverty as an ambitious boy on a subsistence farm. To put it simply, Lincoln mistook strategy for avoidance, and that made him underestimate maneuver and overrate marching directly toward the enemy. As much as anything, that misunderstanding lay at the root of Lincoln's difficulties with McClellan.

The frontier, as historian Charles Grier Sellers has explained, was lazy. With no transportation network, the rewards of hard work would only rot in the fields. There was no incentive to work hard in order to produce a surplus, and the frontiersmen did not. Instead, they went hunting and fishing and moved westward looking for more fertile fields. They did not realize that it was transportation infrastructure and economic development, not more and better land, that would solve their problem. The whole spectacle exasperated Lincoln, who alone among his family felt real ambition. The best study of this problem of Lincoln's early life is also the best book written about Lincoln in my generation, Gabor S. Boritt's *Lincoln and the Economics of the American Dream*.

Lincoln was an ambitious boy, and no one around him was ambitious—not his family and not most of the lazy and restlessly migrating frontiersmen in Indiana and Illinois. Because he eventually rose to success from such a discouraging environment, Lincoln preferred to confront obstacles instead of avoiding them. He thought one ought to make the most of what one had and not keep looking for something better in the West. This is evident in a chilling letter Lincoln wrote in 1851 to his indolent stepbrother, who was considering a move to Missouri in search of economic rewards he had not found on the prairies of Illinois. Lincoln gave him an unforgettable lecture on life:

> I . . . can not but think such a notion is utterly foolish. What can you do in Missouri, better than here? Is the land any richer? Can you there, any more than here, raise corn, & wheat & oats, without work? Will any body there, any more than here, do your work for you? If you intend to go to work, there is no better place than right where you are; if you do not intend to go to work, you can not get along any where. Squirming & crawling about from place to place can do no good.

Lincoln gave the same advice, but with less cruelty and more presidential finesse, to McClellan on April 9, 1862. Exasperated that McClellan would not move forward to engage the enemy with the enormous military organization he had forged in the long months after the Battle of Bull Run (Manassas), Lincoln wrote:

> It is indispensable to you that you strike a blow. I am powerless to help you. You will do me the justice to remember I always insisted, that going down the [Chesapeake] Bay in search of a field, instead of fighting at or near Manassas, was only shifting, and not surmounting, a difficulty—that we would find the same

enemy, and the same, or equal, intrenchments, at either place.

By contrast, when in 1864 Lincoln explained why he was going to leave General Ulysses S. Grant alone and let him make his own military decisions without interference from the president, he noted that "procrastination on the part of commanders" had motivated his interfering in the past.

The commander-in-chief also admired Grant's penchant for "hard desperate fighting." In his period of dismay with McClellan's strategic approach to defeating the Confederacy, Lincoln wrote a memorandum on furloughs, not precisely dated, which stated: "The army, like the nation, has become demoralized by the idea that the war is to be ended, the nation united, and the peace restored, by strategy, and not by hard desperate fighting." Lincoln always wished to avoid misguided violence on civilians, but when it came to the enemy's organized armies, Lincoln was not combat shy. He had a high tolerance for bloody military struggle and long casualty lists. Lincoln's suspicion of strategy as a form of avoidance probably hastened his generals into combat, but even that idea of meeting and surmounting obstacles was not exactly the same as Lincoln's idea that war necessarily involved "hard, tough fighting that will hurt somebody," as he expressed the idea on another occasion.

Where did Lincoln's rather vigorously bloody military visions come from? They were likely derived from his famous wrestling match with Jack Armstrong in New Salem, Illinois, in 1831. The details vary according to reminiscence, and the sifting of the evidence is well done by Douglas Wilson in *Honor's Voice: The Transformation of Abraham Lincoln* and by Michael Burlingame in *Abraham Lincoln: A Life*. Lincoln had been challenged as a newcomer to town by the local bullies, called the Clary's Grove Boys, to a wrestling match with their champion, Jack Armstrong. There was controversy over whether Lincoln had used an unsportsmanlike chokehold during the brutal wrestling match. But the outcome in most recollections was that Lincoln acquitted himself well, and because of that he gained the respect and leadership aura he retained ever after among common men. Historians tend to agree that the episode was a turning point for Lincoln.

Years later, Lincoln thought of battle as a big wrestling

Abraham Lincoln. Washington, D.C., 1865. Photographer Alexander Gardner. Library of Congress Prints and Photographs Division.

match—with not much science to it. Here is the best evidence: at one point in August 1864, while Grant was besieging Petersburg, Grant received a panicky communication from General Henry W. Halleck suggesting the need to divert as many as 20,000 soldiers to the home front to pacify resistance to the draft rumored to be brewing. Grant did not want to do it and thought any such domestic trouble could be handled by the state militias. When Lincoln saw this correspondence, he could not help injecting himself into the conversation. He sent Grant a memorably terse telegram on August 17, 1864: "I have seen your dispatch expressing your unwillingness to break your hold where you are. Neither am I willing. Hold on with a bull-dog grip . . . and chew & choke, a much as possible." The terms "bulldog grip" and "chew and choke" recall the imagery of the wrestling match in New Salem of 33 years earlier. Once again, Lincoln's early experiences determined the later man's statesmanship and strategy.

Like James McPherson, most military historians focus on Lincoln's "steep learning curve" as commander-in-chief in the Civil War. But he did not have to grow as much or as fast as this modern understanding suggests. The talk in modern biographies of Lincoln's "capacity for growth" is not very helpful in understanding him as a constitutionalist or as commander-in-chief. Many of his greatest qualities, ideas, and attitudes even in the realm of military thought were present almost from the beginning. Colin R. Ballard, the British writer who was among the first to recognize the "military genius" of Abraham Lincoln was right to use the term "genius" in the title of his book, as though military talent were an innate quality. "Like the poet," he wrote, "the strategist is born, not made, and Lincoln had the character of a born strategist." It is time to reconsider Abraham Lincoln's life from its hardscrabble start to its brilliant finish in Civil War victory as the product of genius and not of growth.

## Sources

Direct quotations from Lincoln come from the indispensable source, Roy P. Basler, ed., *The Collected Works of Abraham Lincoln*, 9 vols. (Rutgers University Press, 1953–55). The similarly indispensable and complex modern view of Lincoln's youth comes from Gabor S. Boritt, *Lincoln and the Economics of the American Dream*, orig. pub. 1978 (University of Illinois Press, 1994), from Michael Burlingame, *Abraham Lincoln: A Life*, 2 vols. (Johns Hopkins University Press, 2008), and from Douglas L. Wilson, *Honor's Voice: The Transformation of Abraham Lincoln* (Alfred A. Knopf, 1998).

Crucial original sources for his early life appear in Douglas L. Wilson and Rodney O. Davis, *Herndon's Informants: Letters,*

*Interviews, and Statements about Abraham Lincoln* (University of Illinois Press, 1998). Boritt also recognized that Lincoln's post-Fredericksburg conversation with Stoddard was important. See also Burlingame, *Dispatches from Lincoln's White House: The Anonymous Civil War Journalism of Presidential Secretary William O. Stoddard* (University of Nebraska Press, 2002). There are insights on the frontier in Charles Grier Sellers, *The Market Revolution: Jacksonian America, 1815–1846* (Oxford University Press, 1991). Boritt argued that Lincoln was little interested in national expansion because of his experience with westward-moving frontiersmen.

On Lincoln as commander-in-chief, see James M. McPherson, *Tried by War: Abraham Lincoln as Commander in Chief* (Penguin, 2008). For an excellent modern study that takes as its theme Lincoln's growth see Eric Foner, *The Fiery Trial: Abraham Lincoln and American Slavery* (W.W. Norton, 2010). The title of this essay and the quotation on genius in the conclusion come from Colin R. Ballard, *The Military Genius of Abraham Lincoln* (World, 1952, orig. pub. 1926). The significance of Lincoln's phrase "the better angels of our nature" is magnified in the title of Steven Pinker's *The Better Angels of Our Nature: Why Violence Has Declined* (Viking, 2011).

Jefferson Finis Davis. 1858–1860. Photographer Mathew B. Brady. Library of Congress Prints and Photographs Division.

# Jefferson Davis as War Leader

WILLIAM J. COOPER

As president of the Confederate States of America, Jefferson Davis led his country in its war against the United States. The Confederate Constitution followed the U.S. Constitution in giving the president the basic powers of commander-in-chief. Thus, in wartime the Confederate president would lead the political and military effort. Davis certainly possessed the requisite qualifications to become commander-in-chief, a war leader. Indeed, few who have led this nation in war from the War of 1812 to Iraq could match his pedigree. He had military, political, and administrative experience that set him apart from other southern notables in 1861.

Davis's particular background was immensely influential in his selection as provisional president of the fledgling Confederacy. He had graduated from West Point, spent seven years on active duty as an officer in the regular army, and had a distinguished combat record as a regimental commander during the Mexican War. Additionally, he had been a member of both the U.S. House and Senate, serving in the latter body during the 1850s as chairman of the Committee on Military Affairs. Furthermore, between 1853 and 1857 he held the office of secretary of war under President Franklin Pierce.

Despite these impressive credentials, Davis has usually been harshly judged by historians in his starring role, president of the Confederate States. This historical assessment almost makes a prima facie case for disregarding prior achievement and experience in awarding high and responsible office. When Davis is matched against his wartime opposite, Abraham Lincoln, he invariably comes in second—usually a distant second. Yet trailing Lincoln does not automatically brand Davis a failure, for Lincoln was the greatest war leader in our history.

But even when viewed alone, Davis commonly receives poor marks. Without going into an extended historiographical discussion, it is safe to say that most historians have been and still are quite critical of the Confederate president. In general they portray him as brittle, ill-tempered, and unable or unwilling to grow with responsibility. According to this portrayal, these shortcomings were especially disastrous in his inability to appreciate the political dimensions of the war he was fighting and in his micromanagement of his generals.

Before assessing Davis as war leader, it is essential to begin with the criteria used to judge an individual's performance as war leader. Three criteria are central: first, understanding the political and strategic reality facing the country at war; second, articulating war goals or aims in relevant and understandable terms and communicating them to the citizenry; and third, managing the war as the military commander-in-chief. Considering how Davis performed in each of these areas will provide a perspective for assessing him as a war leader.

Jefferson Davis was convinced that an armed struggle between the South, striving for independence, and the North, resisting it, would be long and bitter. From his tenure as secretary of war and as a leader in the U.S. Senate, Davis understood the potential war-making power of the North, both human and material. The formation of the Confederate States of America did not alter his outlook. When hostilities began only two months after his inauguration as provisional president, he acted accordingly. Expecting a lengthy conflict in which the Confederates "would have many a bitter experience," he called on Congress to accept enlistments for the duration of the coming war, or at least three years. In contrast, congressmen, confident of a short, happy war, wanted only six months of service. Despite his urging, Davis could get but one year as a compromise.

As the war progressed, he moved smartly to try to make his side more competitive. Two examples of his actions, one from early in the war and another from late, should make the point. In the spring of 1862, Davis proposed and obtained from Congress the first national conscription act in American history. Then in the final winter of the war, he moved against considerable opposition to sever the powerful southern bond that had bound black slavery to white liberty. Davis successfully advocated putting slaves in Confederate uniforms, realizing that such an act would mean emancipation, at least for slave soldiers, and fundamentally alter southern society. But he was willing to jettison slavery to save Confederate independence.

Davis also comprehended that material limitations sharply restricted his military options. Early on, many Confederates clamored for their troops to take the offensive, to take the war to the enemy and to enemy territory. Davis agreed in principle but recognized that he could not equip his armies for such an undertaking. He could see no good in announcing that the Confederacy had shifted to the offensive when he could not back up such words with actions. He explained that to his generals but not to the Confederate public. Even in the face of criticism, he did not think he could explain his reasoning. "I have borne reproach in silence because to reply by an exact statement of the facts would have exposed our weakness to the enemy." Davis could only "pine for the day when our soil shall be free from invasion and our banners float over the fields of the Enemy." Reality governed.

Fathoming the position of his country involved more than objectivity concerning military resources. From the outset Davis understood that he led a nation in the making, that Confederate nationalism was being constructed during the war. In the autumn of 1861, he urged brigading troops by state because he saw "state pride" as "the highest incentive for gallant and faithful service."

Moreover, he perceived that the fragility of Confederate nationalism, even Confederate loyalty, must govern military strategy. Davis felt that he must temper the military maxim of concentration. The president believed that he had to maintain a visible military presence throughout the country or he would face "dissatisfaction, distress, desertion of soldiers, and opposition of State Govts." In 1863 he wrote one of his commanders: "the general truth, that power is increased by the concentration of an army, is, under our peculiar circumstances subject to modification. The

18 / *Leadership and Generalship in the Civil War*

White House of the Confederacy, residence of Jefferson Davis. Richmond, Virginia, 1865. Photographer John Reekie. Library of Congress Prints and Photographs Division.

evacuation of any portion of territory involves not only the loss of supplies, but in eve[ry] instance . . . troops." Davis could envision a reaction so vigorous that it could cause the disintegration of the Confederacy. He struggled constantly with the vexing problem of concentration of forces.

This tenuous nationalism did not shake Davis's conviction about the ultimate outcome, for he looked to the American Revolution as the cauldron of American nationalism. Although admitting in a public address in January 1863 that war was utterly evil, the president defined "the severe crucible" as essential, for it alone could "cement us together." He went on to say, "the sacrifices we have been subjected to in common, and the glory which encircles our brow has made us a band of brothers, and, I trust, we will be united forever." Now, he asserted, soldiers of every state had become "linked in the defense of a most sacred cause." To him the war was creating Confederate nationalism.

For President Davis, his new country had a single major goal: independence. He viewed the Confederacy as engaged in a struggle matching that of the Founding Fathers—liberty versus despotism. He proclaimed in his inaugural address as provisional president that the Confederacy "illustrate[d] the American idea that governments rest upon the consent of the governed, and that it is the right of the people to alter or abolish governments whenever they become destructive of the ends for which they were established." He emphasized to his fellow Confederates that they were defending the rights they had inherited from their Revolutionary ancestors. Throughout the war he accentuated the intimate relationship between the patriots of the founding generation and the patriots endeavoring to create the southern nation.

As a seasoned professional politician before 1861, Davis was aware that public support was necessary for the success of public policy as well as for the success of a public official. His emphasis on liberty and the sacred link between two generations of founders certainly resonated with his constituency. Southerners had been evangels for liberty and the holiness of the Revolution since the Founding Fathers. Davis pointed to the roster of southern heroes from George Washington forward who had defended liberty. Now under the Confederate banner, their sons and daughters were emulating their example.

In this clarion call to defend liberty, Davis did not dodge slavery. He knew the peculiar institution was at the center of southern society, of the Confederate States. Even so, he insisted that he was not directing a war for slaveowners but for white liberty. White southerners understood perfectly, for at least since the Revolution they had considered their liberty inextricably tied to black slavery. To them, only southern whites could make decisions about slavery; any outsider interfering with the institution threatened white liberty.

In this context Davis stood on traditional southern ground when he condemned Lincoln's Emancipation Proclamation. He interpreted this edict as a manifestation of the brutal war being waged against the Confederacy. He asserted that his government had thwarted all efforts by an aggressive United States. Unable to vanquish "a people determined to be free," the Union, according to Davis, had turned to barbarity, even including the possibility of massacre in the countryside and a horrendous race war, which to the minds of white southerners would be the inevitable result of any general slave uprising. In Davis's judgment the alternatives faced by the Confederates were stark: victory and liberty or defeat and enslavement.

Although Davis clung to liberty as the Confederate goal, he responded to a changing war. By 1863 the course of the struggle had brought real hardship to much of the home front. In his holy quest for liberty, Davis led the Confederacy in directions inconceivable in 1861. He told southerners that they must fight for liberty, no matter the cost. From conscription to enlisting slave soldiers, Davis asked for the previously unthinkable. But he was no dictator. He led but also heard and heeded both leaders and private citizens in an effort to ensure that government policy did not stray too far from public opinion. For example, the president listened to the outcries against the substitution provision of the conscription law, which permitted a drafted man to escape service by paying for a substitute; to critics it allowed the rich to avoid serving and arrayed class against class. In 1863, with Davis's support, the Confederate Congress repealed substitution and even made those who had purchased substitutes eligible for service. The United States had a similar substitution provision, but it remained in place for the entire war. As a veteran of antebellum Mississippi politics, Davis well knew the political danger of even seeming to favor the rich. He envisioned no rich man's war with poor men doing the fighting. Tax policy also shifted. Congress enacted a progressive income tax and placed a 10 percent tax in kind on agricultural products, with the proceeds to be distributed among soldiers' families.

In addition, the president hailed efforts by states and localities to assist those deprived by war. The Confederacy did fall short of fulfilling the needs for assistance, yet seven decades before the New Deal and under extremely difficult circumstances, it tried, however stumblingly. For Davis and his administration, significant relief could only come when battlefield success could relieve pressure on the home front.

From all the letters that crossed his desk, the president had no doubt about the profound sacrifices many Confederates were making. In his public statements, especially by 1864, he always praised their commitment and devotion to the cause, though he admitted he could not predict "how many sacrifices it may take" to achieve victory. Acknowledging in 1864 that many soldiers had absented themselves from the army, Davis never cast aspersions on their patriotism. He realized that these men had gone to war to protect liberty and defend home and family. Yet by late 1863, with home and family often undefended while confronting privation, social disorganization, and advancing Federal armies, many soldiers rethought their primary duty.

Davis understood what was happening and was not impervious to such motivations. Examining the files of men sentenced to death for desertion made a powerful impression. In one case a soldier left his unit upon being informed that the enemy had driven his wife and children from their home; they were all sick and destitute, and one child had already died. This husband and father departed without permission, though he did return, whereupon a court-martial convicted him of desertion. Noting that he would have acted precisely as the soldier did, the president set aside the conviction and ordered the man restored to the ranks. Faced regularly with this hard reality, Davis urged those who had gone home to return to their units. Homes and families could ultimately be protected, he maintained, only by battlefield success. In his mind there was but a single alternative: "slavish submission to despotic usurpation."

As president, Davis strove to get his message before the Confederate public. His formal messages to Congress along with proclamations appeared in newspapers, as did public addresses. Yet he went further. On three occasions—in the winter of 1862–63, in the fall of 1863, and in the fall of 1864—he traveled from the capital of Richmond across much of his country, on the first two occasions all the way to Mississippi, on the third to Alabama. These trips had a military purpose, for he visited with armies and their commanders. But he also met with civilian authorities and with the public. Davis made countless public appearances and delivered numerous speeches, from formal presentations before legislatures to impromptu remarks at railroad stops. He did not hide in Richmond but tried to make himself seen and heard by his fellow citizens.

On the whole he succeeded. Although a multitude of political adversaries slashed at him, especially from 1863 on, no single politician rose to seriously challenge his leadership. His shrill opponents howled, but they accomplished little. These men were strongest in Georgia, where inveterate antagonists Governor Joseph Brown and Vice President Alexander Stephens led the assault. Still, the people of Georgia remained stalwart for the president. As late as 1864 Brown and Stephens failed to turn the state legislature against Davis. Until the bitter end he remained the dominant political force in the Confederacy.

While Davis never shunned his role as leader of the Confederate people and nation, he took quite seriously his position as commander-in-chief of the armed forces. The president considered himself an expert on military matters and believed himself eminently qualified to command an army or to command commanders. He never doubted his own military ability or judgment. In directing the Confederate war, Davis adopted hands-on tactics. His own predilection as well as his sense of duty involved him in all aspects of the military, from the trivial, such as complaints from junior officers, to the deadly serious, such as critical strategic decisions. His administrative style dated to his time as U.S. secretary of war. Then presiding over a small establishment, he wanted to know about everything and see every document. He brought that same practice to the Confederate presidency. Nothing changed, not even by 1862, when he was directing a great war. The minutiae that received his regular attention utterly boggles the mind. He questioned nominations for junior officers and involved himself in deciding whether two pieces of artillery went to the navy or to Charleston. A letter from a captain wanting a transfer from Virginia to the Mississippi Valley received presidential attention. The list is unending.

Davis was his own secretary of war. While he did have men in that office, all but one quite able, he did not create areas of responsibility nor did he delegate authority. He wished for advice, often requesting it, and willingly discussed issues, large and small, but he made the decisions. Although directives that left Richmond carried various signatures, including at times that of the secretary of war, all contained decisions made by Jefferson Davis. Running the war office or the high command, Davis was a micromanager.

Custom House, standing among the ruins. Richmond, Virginia, 1865. Library of Congress Prints and Photographs Division.

Yet he did not deal with his generals in the field in the same manner. Although he appointed the general officers who commanded his armies, once he put them in place, he rarely told them what to do. His instructions in June 1861 to General Joseph E. Johnston at Harpers Ferry set the tone. Informing the general that he wanted Harpers Ferry held as long as possible, the president said that as commander on the scene, Johnston must exercise his own discretion. Likewise, three months later Davis acted similarly when, against the president's wishes, Major General Leonidas Polk violated Kentucky's neutrality by occupying Columbus. There was an immediate political backlash; an alarmed governor of Tennessee warned the president that Polk's move harmed the Confederate cause in Kentucky. Davis then countermanded Polk, but the general insisted that his actions were militarily indispensable. Responding, Davis asserted that "the necessity must justify the action," which meant Polk, the commander on the scene, would make the final decision. He stayed in Kentucky.

Davis pursued that policy throughout the war, though he would recommend courses of action. In the spring of 1862, he suggested to General Albert Sidney Johnston that he isolate one element of the enemy and inflict a mighty blow. But the decision was Johnston's. Again, in the winter of 1862–63, he urged Lieutenant General Theophilus Holmes in Arkansas to assist Joseph Johnston in Mississippi but tempered his language by telling Holmes that he must use his own discretion. Additional examples could be brought forth. It is difficult to explain the contrast between Davis's handling of his field commanders and his management of the war department. The difference was certainly not because he failed to comprehend the change wrought by the telegraph. Throughout the war he utilized that instrument, fully aware that it permitted rapid communication between him and his generals. Perhaps it came from his military background—generals should be left alone. Possibly his service in Mexico with General Zachary Taylor, whom he admired extravagantly, influenced him, for Taylor growled about interference from civilian authorities above him. Whatever the reasons, Davis gave his generals enormous leeway.

Not only did Davis fail to direct his generals, but he too often left them in command long after they should have been removed. Unlike Lincoln, Davis did not regularly relieve generals. Of course, one of the most famous incidents involving Davis and his generals was his firing of Joseph Johnston in 1864 before Atlanta. Yet that action did not occur because Johnston failed to obey orders from Richmond, but instead because he refused to tell Davis what he, Johnston, intended to do. Even so, this is the exception that proves the rule.

A much more common situation prevailed after the failed Confederate advance into Kentucky in 1862. Confederate misfortune in Kentucky came from several directions. At the same time, the inability of Confederate commanders to cooperate was surely crucial. Following the Confederate withdrawal, the three senior generals—two army commanders, Edmund Kirby Smith and Braxton Bragg, and Bragg's ranking subordinate, Leonidas Polk—all blamed each other for the outcome. Davis thought highly of each officer, considering all of them loyal, selfless patriots. He saw them as he had earlier described Smith to Bragg: "He has taken every position without the least tendency to question its advantage to himself, without complaint when his prospects for distinction were remote, and with alacrity when danger and hardships were to be met." Yet the failure in Kentucky terribly disappointed the president. As a result he brought the three men individually to Richmond, where he listened to each deflect responsibility and accuse the others. After hearing these recriminations, Davis, incredibly, left the three in place, even promoting Smith and Polk, and implored them for the good of the cause to get along. When fundamental overhaul was desperately needed, Davis stood still.

And there were other examples of this kind of response or nonresponse. For the possibility of the ultimate Confederate success, they happened far too frequently. In such instances, for all the right reasons, a ruthless, even pragmatic, commander-in-chief would have instituted dramatic changes, including dismissals, transfers, and promotion of junior generals. In the Army of Tennessee, the cancer that Davis did not even attempt to excise in the post-Kentucky weeks was left to grow even more virulent.

Jefferson Davis as a war leader performed far more ably in his political role than in his military one. Concerning the political dimensions of his position, broadly construed, he merits high marks. On the military side the result is mixed. Davis did comprehend the strategic situation facing his country, and his basic strategic decisions were reasonable and understandable. But as a purely military commander-in-chief, he exhibited serious flaws. Too often he did not exercise appropriate command authority over generals or intervene effectively when crippling disagreements divided senior commanders. Simply put, Davis did not have the steel or ruthlessness to make absolutely essential command decisions.

Originally published in William J. Cooper, Jr., *Jefferson Davis and the Civil War Era*, Louisiana State University Press, 2008.

Unveiling of Lee Monument. Richmond, Virginia, 1890. From B. E. Andrews, *History of the United States*. Charles Scribner's Sons, 1912.

# Lee and His Detractors in the Age of the Anti-Hero

Robert K. Krick

Thirty years after the Civil War, time had worked on Confederate veterans' recollections. It had smoothed away some of the sectional rancor and some of the suffering, brightening recollections of 1860s adventures and dulling recollections of 1860s anguish.

The late-Victorian era featured a zeitgeist eagerly attuned to romantic imagery and emotive language. Much turn-of-the-century literature ran to purple prose and hyperbole; Generals John B. Gordon and Joshua L. Chamberlain exemplify the genre. In Gordon's pages, no soldier died in mortal agony; instead, a speeding lead messenger freed his warrior soul to join fellow heroes in Valhalla. Chamberlain's egocentric narrative spared very little space for anyone but himself; when it did, the scene played out as a sort of chivalric medieval joust.

The taste for that kind of prose faded long ago, leaving behind skepticism about the legitimacy of tales described so vividly, especially vintage 1890–1920. Still, most of Gordon's exploits stand up to scrutiny, their framing notwithstanding. There were many who claimed to have been promoted personally by Lee but whose papers were "lost" during the Appomattox campaign. A list of such soldiers would fill volumes; so would obituaries of Confederates praised as faithful until the surrender—but whose official service records contain AWOL slips and Federal oaths signed in 1864 or even 1863.

Individual claims of rank mushroomed in the postwar

transmogrification. Early in the 20th century, a pundit suggested that it was wise always to refer to any adult male south of Wilmington, Delaware, as "colonel," unless you knew for sure that he preferred "judge." After the war, a mayoral candidate in Richmond who had served with Parker's Virginia Battery as a private boasted of that rank, and then joked that he may have been the only private soldier in the entire Army of Northern Virginia.

Bragging on a war record, not always accurately nor modestly, in quest of political preferment, became known as "waving the bloody shirt" in the North, but of course the phenomenon roamed the South as well. Colonel Frederick W. M. Holliday could not have become governor of Virginia in 1877, observers suggested, had he not lost an arm at Cedar Mountain. The orator proposing General Francis R. T. Nicholls, who had lost an arm at Winchester and a leg at Chancellorsville, for governor of Louisiana in 1876, said, "I nominate all that is left of General Nicholls." During the campaign, a similarly mangled soldier picked up the note: "What's left of me is going to vote for what's left of General Nicholls."

Holliday and Nicholls had plenty of service on which to boast; many another claimant did not. A few years ago, a careful researcher examined the self-proclaimed last surviving Confederate veterans. When "the last Confederate survivor" died, ostensibly a veteran of the renowned Texas Brigade, it was easy to establish that he was a fraud. In fact, every one of those claims was bogus, those late survivors having been lured by flattering publicity and the prospect of a pension during the Depression. Significantly, the investigation established similar results for the last elderly pseudo-veterans of Union armies. Soldiers grown old sometimes ramble away from reliability, often very far indeed, whatever their longitude. The trend, while not surprising, nicely highlights the problem of late-life fantasy and mendacity.

Tendentious modern historians insist that the rosy glow infusing the Lost Cause is somehow unique. They go further to identify it as the conscious, manipulative creation of a defeated people. According to this line of thinking, Robert E. Lee was not really all that popular during the war. He only became an icon when carefully created as one after the war, having been chosen by Machiavellian conspirators to meet the need for a Southern Hero.

Thomas Connelly's inaugural book about the hollow, artificial

Lee legend declares, "Not until the 1880s would Lee be regarded as the South's invincible general." At his death, "This eminence lay years ahead." Ten years later William Piston said about the same thing: "When he died on October 12, 1870, Lee was only one of a large number of Confederate heroes," and clearly behind some of them. Another decade later Carol Reardon wrote: "Virginians directed postwar efforts to recast Robert E. Lee as the Confederacy's great hero."

The immense body of war-date adulation of Lee seems impossible to ignore. The 20th-century philosophical construction, "Hanlon's Razor"—a sort of corollary to the widely cited Occam's Razor, by a 14th-century logician—explains how anyone could miss that evidence. Never attribute to malice, Hanlon's Razor posits, what can be adequately explained by ignorance or sloth.

Ignoring or denying the praise of countless thousands of Confederates who hymned Lee's stature during the war seems startling. Is such denial driven by malice? Or by ignorance and sloth? Perhaps. The virtually unrelated question of whether Lee deserved the adulation falls into latitudes subjective enough to defy adamant declaration. That the adulation flowed is beyond peradventure. They may have been wrong, those contemporary Confederates, but that they believed it cannot be disputed.

In addition to recognizing a preference for contemporary witness, an important element in looking at evidence about Lee's status during the war (and about everything else as well) is establishing a hierarchy of credibility about witnesses, whatever the date of their testimony. Some people, and some sources of information, deserve more credit than others. The modern tendency to dismiss Confederate accounts as inherently, automatically dishonest ignores that fundamental principle.

Robert Stiles, the Virginian artillerist and field officer, in his widely popular memoir, waxes colorful, quotable, interesting—but not routinely reliable. A contemporary at the University of Virginia wrote that Stiles's enthusiasms reminded him of "a boy who, after flushing a flock of sparrows writes of a great flight of bald eagles he had seen." Henry Kyd Douglas, sometime Stonewall Jackson staff officer, offers even more color and drama and quotability than Stiles and even less reliability.

William Nelson Pendleton, having grown gray in the Episcopal

William Nelson Pendleton. Date unknown. Library of Congress Prints and Photographs Division.

pulpit in Lexington, Virginia, presumably embraced the principle of unswerving honesty as part of donning the surplice. His Civil War narratives, nonetheless, almost always strayed onto a tangent not congruent with facts, indeed very often on a direct reciprocal from simple truth. His imaginative dishonesty about Gettysburg would have served conspirators wonderfully well as texts for pro-Lee crusades; but the general's loyal staffers (e.g., Taylor, Venable, Marshall) did not climb aboard the convenient bandwagon. Instead they stuck to the truth as they saw it. A great many veterans, indeed most of them on both sides, were not devoted to either persiflage or dishonesty.

In vivid contrast with the Pendleton syndrome, Edward Porter Alexander's evidence, voluminous and intelligent, comes close to being unimpeachable. William Allan, who worked at Washington College in Lexington after the war, and made important notes there at first hand, never waxed disingenuous and deserves high marks for reliability. Jedediah Hotchkiss of upstate New York and Staunton, Virginia, held strong opinions, not always accurate, but strove faithfully for truth.

Had the Reverend General Pendleton hewn closer to the truth, or even been unimpeachably accurate, would that make Alexander more believable? Surely not, any more than Alexander's own virtues somehow ought to be considered as an indirect means of polishing Pendleton's reputation for trustworthiness.

As in every analysis of evidence, historical or otherwise, prudent judgment is warranted. To attribute the near-invincible reliability of the crisply authoritative Alexander/Allan/Hotchkiss stripe to all primary sources by Confederate soldiery would be irresponsible. To precisely the same level, tarring all Confederate primary sources as self-serving, dishonest, and undependable, in variations of the Pendleton/Douglas/Stiles mode, would be equally foolish.

A corollary is the scornful rejection of any postwar testimony not corroborated by a contemporary account; proximity to an event of course factors prominently in any evaluation of sources, deserving at least as much weight as any other. For example, some modern historians assert that the dismay of the Confederates who bewailed a lost opportunity at Culp's and Cemetery Hills at Gettysburg on July 1, 1863, was based on hindsight and that the vivid postwar accounts must be part of the all-pervasive Lost Cause bilge. Lee himself summarized the position on February 19, 1870—but of course that was a bit after July 1863. He believed that "if Jackson had been there he would have succeeded."

Contemporary evidence eventually did surface from men on the spot who saw what most felt and happened to write it down in the midst of fighting and marching and struggling. A North Carolina lieutenant writing within days of the battle came to a similar conclusion:

> That delay was fatal to us. . . . We lost the golden opportunity in not keeping up the attack that evening. . . . It is hardly possible to say how great our victory would have been. . . . There we missed the genius of Jackson. The simplest solider in the ranks felt it. . . . But, timidity in the commander that stepped into the shoes of the fearless Jackson, prompted delay.

There remains room to parse the options on the first day at Gettysburg and their potential results; but not to scorn those expressing frustration as having dishonestly invented the feeling.

What of Lee's battlefield attainments, as opposed to Confederate perceptions of their admired leader? Lee, against long odds, crafted some of the most amazing campaigns in all of American history, even of world history. His thorough reversal of the war's course in eight weeks of summer 1862—moving it from the outskirts of Richmond to the doorstep of Washington—is hard to contemplate without some astonishment.

With an army not yet sculpted to his preferences, led by many subordinate officers who soon would be exiled to lesser duties, Lee stood the war squarely on its ear during that summer. It is impossible to imagine Joseph E. Johnston, whose wounding in the twilight on May 31 opened the army command to Lee, achieving anything faintly resembling that military revolution. The tiny bits of metal that hit Johnston that evening had even more to do with the war's course than did the three lead balls that ended Jackson's career eleven months later.

The Second Manassas (Bull Run) campaign, part of the reorientation of the war away from the Southern capital, featured movement and daring unlike anything in earlier campaigns and launched the collaboration between Lee and Jackson, the quintessential executive officer. Each success bolstered the confidence of musket-wielding Southern soldiers, and contributed to a growing feeling among some of their foe that Lee outshone their own leadership.

Chancellorsville, the greatest of Lee's creations and against the greatest odds, simply was incomparable. The salient criticism of his plans there, of excessive aggression at the end of the campaign, wilts under new evidence. Correspondence between Lee and J.E.B. Stuart of May 4–5, 1863, long sequestered at the Huntington Library in California, makes abundantly clear the degree to which

Lee adamantly opposed attacking entrenched Federals, though eager to exploit his enemy's brief vulnerability while re-crossing the Rappahannock. Lee's impact on the soldiery became a priceless national asset—his other considerable attributes aside. On the same May 4 when Lee and Stuart corresponded, the army commander faced the need to take over operations well to the east of Chancellorsville. The portion of his army dealing with John Sedgwick's Federal rearguard there had slipped out of local control.

Seasoned Southern infantry recognized the disarray and stirred restlessly. "I never saw officers & men so utterly and so generally demoralized," wrote Major Richard Watson York of the 6th North Carolina. He confessed, in a letter written in 1872: "I, myself, to some extent, participated" in the demoralization. The major, a college professor, scholarly author, and son of a Duke University founder, was not much prone to sententiousness or hero worship, but described the universal relief when Lee appeared to restore order.

> Suddenly we saw passing through the thin woods . . . Gen. Lee. As soon as his face was well seen . . . the word soon went down the line "All is right, Uncle Robert is here, we will whip them." There was no cheering, the men leaned on their muskets and looked at him . . . as tho' a God were passing by. The safe, implicit confidence in security, the certainty of success, the lifting of the terrible doubt that had hung over us, was more than cap-tossing or shouting.

None of the men near Fredericksburg that afternoon tossed a hat in the air or hollered. The surpassing value of that kind of impact on troops facing mortal combat would be hard to calculate in concrete terms.

Four months after that Chancellorsville episode, James Longstreet achieved the independent command he long had sought, taking the 1st Corps west to Chickamauga and then into east Tennessee. Removed from what he perceived as the stultifying superintendence of Lee, he ran into disaster at Knoxville at the hands of a few score Federals ensconced in Fort Sanders, under the command of the maladroit Ambrose E. Burnside. In attempting to shift blame from himself, Longstreet launched a series of courts martial, which embarrassed him further.

Longstreet's long-nurtured chafing under Lee's command in

Virginia faded in retrospect. He had written to his collaborator Joseph E. Johnston in October 1862 insisting that the army loved Johnston more than Lee; if he would return to the army, even in a subordinate role, within a few months they could contrive to restore him to command in place of Lee. As spring dawned in 1864, after his unsuccessful foray into independent command, Longstreet welcomed his return under Lee. He instructed his wife to name a newborn son for Lee—a remarkable reversal. After Lee died six years later, Longstreet spent more than three decades casting aspersions at the dead man, some of them pungent and vitriolic, earning himself the favor of many modern scholars. Good sense militates against categorizing all of anything, but much of the Longstreet enthusiasm of recent years arises from his status as about the only high-ranking officer to have damned Lee.

In April of 1864, Longstreet's men had no doubt where they stood on the Lee question. One of the most dramatic displays of affection for Lee—for any commander at any time—took place on the 29th at a review that reunited the men and their general. The 1st Corps gathered in a field near Mechanicsville, Virginia—the tiny hamlet just west of Boswell's Tavern, not the better known Mechanicsville of Seven Days battle fame. Dozens of accounts tell of the emotional moment. Abram Hayne Young of the 3rd South Carolina Infantry, fervent but not accoutered with any excess of orthographic sophistication, wrote to his sister:

> Yesterday we had a grand review by the greatest of Generals: Gen'l·R. E. Lee. . . . And after the review was over they all crowded a round the old Gen'l to Shake handes with him. And some Said they had Shuck handes with the gratest general in the world.

Sergeant Young went into the breach with his regiment on May 6, among the first to arrive near the Widow Tapp's Field, and a bullet into his lung laid him low. He died that evening, less than a week after his enthusiastic letter home, and 36 days after his 24th birthday.

Artillerist Alexander, cited above as exemplar of the good-witness option, suffered from no discernible tendency toward hollow sentiment. He was a flinty-eyed narrator, hotly accused after the war of being inadequately respectful to Lee in written analyses.

James Longstreet. c.1861–1865. National Archives and Records Administration.

Contrary to his usual businesslike tenor, Alexander's description of the April reunion waxed deeply emotive:

> the general reins up his horse, & bares his good gray head, & looks at us & we shout & cry & wave our battleflags. . . . Sudden as a wind, a wave of sentiment, such as can only come to large crowds in full sympathy . . . seemed to sweep over the field. Each man seemed to feel the bond which held us all to Lee. There was no speaking, but the effect was that of a military sacrament.

Seven days later, the men who had shouted themselves hoarse at Mechanicsville pounded down the Orange Plank Road in the Wilderness, arriving at the climax of the greatest crisis Lee had yet faced, and redeemed the moment. The military sacrament paid dividends far beyond any consideration of tactics, operations, and strategy—in the Wilderness and on other famous fields.

Lee's perceived persona also worked its way on officers in close contact with him. Although the general's modern detractors tend to consider Lee's facade artificial, even dishonest, contemporaries in contact with the general virtually all came away impressed. Samuel Merrifield Bemiss, a surgeon from Kentucky, tended Lee in the spring of 1863 while Lafayette Guild, the army's regular medical director, was himself absent sick. In writing to his wife and children, Bemiss waxed enthusiastic about Lee in language as emphatic as any postwar manipulator could have fabricated.

> He is so noble a specimen of men that even if he were not so distinguished, you would be attracted by his appearance and manner. . . . Always polite and agreeable, and thinking less of himself than he ought to. . . . I know you would all love him if you saw him, but with a deep quiet admiration which would find expression in a desire to imitate his actions and arrive at his excellencies. . . . On every visit my admiration for him increases.

Bemiss later reported that Lee had recovered from what had ailed him that winter, contradicting the modern notion that his failing health stymied army operations in 1863—an idea circulated primarily in a popular novel, hardly a reliable source.

Quoting Bemiss, Young, York, and Alexander—four witnesses in an army numbering 65,000 men and more—of course proves nothing at all. They are representative, however, of a roaring bore tide of precisely that kind of sentiment, which is unmistakable and pervasive. The primary sources confirm the essential truth of Lee's towering wartime popularity in the South.

Lee's image in Northern ranks also rose during 1862 and 1863, albeit without reflecting the warmth radiating in Southern evaluations. A considerable literature examines that reaction in the Federal armies and decries it as unwonted, albeit unmistakable. In an 1864 column, *New York Times* founder and editor Henry J. Raymond offered a powerful tribute to the prowess of Confederate arms. As a close friend and advisor to Abraham Lincoln and national chairman of the Republican Party, Raymond was an implausible candidate for a role in a sinister 1864 precursor of the Lost Cause conspiracy, but he sounds precisely like what conspiracy theorists decry:

> The rebels have exhibited a most wonderful energy and skill in carrying on their struggle. No people on the face of the earth ever made so hard a fight with such limited means, a combination of dash and endurance never before equaled in military history. All candid men, whatever their hatred of the rebellion . . . are free to admit that the final triumph of our national armies will be due only to superiority in numbers.

Confederates relished their leader's stature across the lines. A North Carolinian named Deaton wrote home that his general was "considered the greatest genius of the age by the Yankees." Lieutenant William G. Hinson of Haskell's 7th South Carolina Cavalry corralled a Federal officer who had escaped from a Richmond prison but got lost in the swamps and was recaptured. Hinson admired the man's "pluck and perseverance" and talked with him about the state of affairs. "If our army had a Lee," the captive grumbled, "we would have been in Richmond long ago." Attitudes like that in both armies obviously redounded to the military advantage of the Army of Northern Virginia.

One manifestation of anti-Lee sentiment amongst modern scholars is the notion that his deeply religious nature revealed personality and psychological disorders. His devout faith pleased auditors in the 1860s and beyond. In the 1970s and down to the present, that faith has been a lynchpin for his detractors. The general's notions of personal worthlessness without God's guidance and support, serve as a text for modern detractors to depict Lee as insecure—this being in chapters adjacent to the ones that paint him arrogant and utterly insensitive.

Scorn for Lee's piety is one of several aspects of the modern attacks on him that seem to be founded in feckless presentism. In the middle of the 19th century, humans who acknowledged God as the source of their own strength and essential to their success stood in the religious mainstream. The idea that a subscriber to that pervasive tenet can be psychoanalyzed as unbalanced and defective does not stand up to serious scrutiny. It is important for historians to avoid applying the current climate intact to a different era or exploiting knowledge of ultimate results. British historian C. V. Wedgwood offers a crisp summary of the notion: "History is lived forwards but it is written in retrospect. We know the end before we consider the beginning and we could never wholly recapture what it was to know the beginning only." The concept seems alien to some of Lee's detractors.

Novelist Philip Roth has written deftly that one of Americans' most fervently embraced communal passions is indulging in an "ecstasy of sanctimony" about their self-defined advancements over others—condemning the moral failings, real and imagined, of others, past and present. I am reminded of the Antinomian heresy that enflamed the first century world (and again in the 16th century, and beyond). It suggested that souls are saved only by grace, so there is no reason to hew to any moral law or to avoid malfeasance. Among the faithful, behavior is irrelevant. In reverse application, Confederates, as secular infidels, cannot redeem themselves from the failing of being on the wrong side. Their testimony—about Lee, and about anything—apparently does not have standing.

A bright youngster from Ohio who loved Civil War sites from his youth, focused on Ohio troops (free of Southern inclinations) and went on many a battlefield tour with me. As a high school student eligible to graduate with honors, he wrote a history paper to meet one of the requirements. He chose to describe the Battle of Fredericksburg. The paper mentioned in passing the Aurora Borealis that bedizened the northern horizon the night after the battle. Southerners, being unfamiliar with the phenomenon because of their home latitudes, marveled about the sight in letters home. Some of them—deeply religious, easily impressed, or perhaps simply fey—theorized that the display was a supernatural indication of celebration for the great Confederate victory.

The teacher graded the paper down because the student had accepted the notion—not that the event had some special meaning, but that the borealis had glowed in the sky at all—since he cited a Confederate source for the tale. A historical premise in far too many instances, apparently considered well worth learning early and holding dear, is that Southerners made things up and cannot be trusted.

In answer to his plea for assistance, I forwarded some Northern and thus unimpeachable accounts of the light show in the heavens on the night of December 14th, 1862. The words of some New Englanders apparently served the purpose, as did reports from an official weather station, operated in Georgetown, D.C., by an "Old School Presbyterian minister" (as self-defined in the 1860 census), and presumably not engaged in a vast conspiracy. The student survived his gaffe, but the snubbing of Confederate sources persists.

George Washington wrote of the wide chasms inevitable between human reactions to the same evidence. In words apposite to all of mankind's differences, Washington wrote thoughtfully:

> Shall I arrogantly pronounce that whosoever differs from me, must discern the subject through a distorting medium, or be influenced by some nefarious scheme? The mind is so formed in different persons as to contemplate the same objects in different points of view. Hence originates the difference on questions of the greatest import, human and divine.

Washington's dictum applies to subjective viewpoints on the records and achievements of Lee. People of powerful minds and contemplative miens may examine the same evidence and reach opposite conclusions. Was Lee's performance at Chancellorsville foolishness redeemed by luck or unparalleled brilliance? Was East Cemetery Hill the key in the fading light of July 1 and within reach or was it an unattainable phantasm? Those subjective calls, and almost everything we perceive and conclude in our quotidian existence, produce variable reactions. In the objective matter of weighing Lee's war-time popularity, deserved or not, I would submit that Hanlon's Razor offers the only real multiple choice for those denying the patent truth: malice, ignorance, sloth—or all of the above in rich admixture.

Millions of words are preserved from Lee's own pen, together with countless more from his intimates and contemporaries. There is no need for anyone to accept as the immutable conclusion any particular assessment of Lee. The opulent array of contemporary writings makes it easy for someone who cares to see it all without intermediary or interference. There always will be a great many people, including those raised without any hint of precedential Southern propinquity, who will read and muse and marvel—and come away impressed, and attached, and eager to learn more.

Robert E. Lee on Traveller. c1866. From a photograph by Michael Miley. Library of Congress Prints and Photographs Division.

# Robert E. Lee and the Three Obligations of Command

Carol Reardon

As such books as *Robert E. Lee on Leadership*, *The Leadership Lessons of Robert E. Lee*, and *The Ethical Leadership of Robert E. Lee* attest, the great Confederate chieftain has become a favorite model for leadership and management specialists. In their hands, the great captain's command of the Army of Northern Virginia in a high-risk environment marked by volatility, uncertainty, complexity, and ambiguity can instruct, inspire, and even entertain. But such works usually find shelf space in the business section of the bookstore, and are the product of adroit cherrypicking through Marse Robert's long and fascinating nineteenth-century life for the purpose of illuminating specific points in some twenty-first century leadership philosophy.

But Lee still has much to teach us about leadership if we respect historical context and evaluate his leadership against the expectations of his own time. From the first day he donned a uniform, Lee became part of—and never apart from—a military institution with its own unique professional culture. What did that culture teach Lee about commanding an army?

The answer is straightforward: not much. The antebellum U.S. Army had no schools for generals. West Point graduates such as Lee obtained a scientific and military education, heavy on engineering and company-level tactics of the combat arms, most appropriate to their early career assignments. Cadets took no more than nine lessons on the operation of armies in campaign and the generals who commanded them. Moreover, they took those classes during the spring of their last year, amid the distractions of impending graduation and commissioning. The substance of most of those lessons came from translated European military treatises heralding the accomplishments of Frederick the Great or Napoleon; the U.S. Army possessed little such professional military literature of its own. For those soldiers who continued to study their profession after graduation—and Lee did—their European texts taught that successful generalship rested on two main qualities: character and competence.

Character always trumped competence. Swiss military theorist Antoine Henri Jomini, one of the leading military authors of the day, wrote that "the character of the man is above all other requisites in a commander-in-chief" of an army. The essence of character, that prime military virtue, could be captured in a single word: courage. A good general, wrote Jomini, first must possess "a high moral courage, capable of great resolutions." Second, he must show "a physical courage which takes no account of danger."

A good general somehow—through self-study, experience, or even formal schooling—also had to master the principles of war, but, beyond that, wrote Jomini, it was "not necessary that he be a man of vast erudition." But history's greatest commanders stood apart from the merely good ones in possessing one additional and extraordinarily rare trait: the innate quality of genius. When an opportunity arose or a crisis loomed, a general possessed of genius immediately comprehended its complexity, defined a desirable end-state, designed a plan of action—or multiple plans—each marked by boldness and creativity, and energetically ensured their successful execution. No one could teach genius. A military genius was born, not made.

Thus, Lee came to his professional maturity likely understanding the kind of man a successful general must *be* and the specific body of military knowledge he must *know*. But Lee's books seldom told him how to translate character and competence into practical and effective courses of action. Military writers explained in detail the dangers of river crossings and the challenges of marching through forests or defiles and establishing encampments—actions most often left to captains or colonels in the field—but they did not supply similarly detailed instructions to generals on how to win a war. Instead, they worked from the premise that a general possessing genius for high command already knew what needed to be done. Everyone else simply had to try their best to apply the principles of war as best they could within individual limitations.

So, where does Lee fit into all of this? He was far too modest, of course, to claim genius. Instead, let us consider Lee in appropriate historical context. As a soldier, he belonged to an army, a complex hierarchical organization. For that army to function at top effectiveness, each soldier, regardless of rank, must continually meet three obligations, whether on the battlefield or on the training ground, on the march or in camp, in routine discharge of duty or moments of great crisis. A good soldier would act steadily and positively to: (1) support his superiors' efforts, (2) support his own efforts, and (3) support his subordinates' efforts to achieve a shared goal. How—and how well—did Robert E. Lee meet these obligations?

First, how did Lee support his superiors? He did so in many ways. As Jomini had written, the first care of a commander upon taking the field "should be to agree with the head of the state upon the character of the war." From the first day he donned the gray, Lee made clear to Davis his unequivocal support for the president's desired political endstate: independence. He always respected a founding premise of American civil-military relations: the primacy of civilian control over the military. Even as his military authority grew, Lee remained Davis's exemplary follower. Lee's correspondence with civilian superiors included frequent reaffirmations of his willingness to respect their decisions and to refrain from military actions they deemed incompatible with larger political initiatives. He even counseled generals recently commissioned directly from the civilian world to adhere to their new obligations as "military men" and to respect the chain of command and "obey the President's orders."

Much of Lee's continued success in supporting the efforts of his political superiors also rested on superior interpersonal communication skills. As Davis's military advisor in the spring of 1862, Lee especially understood the president's preference for detailed and frequent updates in crisis situations. Thus, after he assumed command of the Army of Northern Virginia on the outskirts of Richmond in June 1862, Lee immediately began to work in concert with Davis's preferences. "Our position requires you should know everything & you must excuse my troubling you" became a recurring theme in Lee's frequent updates during the Seven Days battles. As Davis's confidence in Lee's judgment grew, however, Lee could begin his messages during his operations in Maryland in September 1862 with: "When you do not hear from me, you may feel sure that I do not think it necessary to trouble you." Surprisingly, Davis did not balk, satisfied that Lee would report important news immediately.

Clearly, the open channel of communication helped to foster a shared trust that allowed the two men—neither particularly open by nature—to enjoy frank exchanges on matters that quickly extended well beyond the limits of Lee's formal authority. While Davis had good reason to believe himself to be as well-informed on military affairs as any American political leader or general of his time, the concept of military "strategy" itself was still in its infancy. Jomini had defined it simply as "war on the map," military operations beyond the battlefield. The theorists of the era generally limited their discussions of strategy almost exclusively to the military sphere. But such a narrow definition proved too simplistic for the complexities of a conflict on the scope and scale of the Civil War. Davis needed at least a few knowledgeable and trusted advisors such as Lee to help him think them through.

To a degree most assuredly underappreciated, Lee did just that. He freely provided input on many elements of national military policy. He offered well-informed critiques of legislation on military organization, and he advised Davis on personnel matters ranging from conscription to general officer assignments that potentially impacted the fortunes of Confederate forces well beyond his own Army of Northern Virginia. He also tried hard to keep himself current on the actions of all Confederate armies, not merely his own, and applied the principles of war—especially concentration of effort—to guide the direction of military operations in all of the Confederacy's interconnected theaters of war.

Lee helped Davis to discern essential from peripherally important efforts, and to decide if, how, when, and where to shift supplies or troops—even away from Lee's own army, at times—to the front in greatest need. While he certainly looked out for his own army's best interests, he did not suffer quite so badly from the

Virginia "myopia" that some critics have attributed to him.

Lee also advised Davis, and occasionally the sitting secretary of war, on diplomatic, economic, political and social matters, aspects of national life well outside the recognized sphere of professional expertise expected of his generation of soldiers. Lee wrote to state governors to encourage cooperation with national military manpower initiatives. In expansive exchanges with Richmond, Lee considered at length the importance of protecting civilian morale and respecting private property on the Southern home front and bemoaned the inequity of sacrifice between the battlefront and the home front. He discussed the mixed prospects for influencing Northern antiwar sentiment before key national and state elections. He offered suggestions for systematizing railroad repair, for encouraging entrepreneurial spirit, and for labor reforms to supply workers for nitre caves.

Lee and Davis discussed the implications of fluctuations in the New York gold market during the summer campaign of 1864, and Lee shared with the president his frustration with the French and British for continuing to view the war as "between a party contending for abstract slavery and the other against it," while entirely ignoring the "vital rights involved."

Davis even asked Lee whether or not he thought it advisable to reestablish the Society of the Cincinnati in the Confederacy, recalling heated public criticism of the exclusive organization open only to officers of the Continental Army and their male descendents. Protests during the early Republic had centered on the creation of an artificial aristocracy or a military elite. Lee decided against it, lest it stoke class tensions that might undermine a common commitment to the goal of independence.

Late in the war, Lee offered support for raising black troops for military service; he also ruminated on the consequences of such a course upon traditional Southern society. Lee's usefulness to Davis covered such breadth that it is no wonder that Davis once wrote him, "I need your counsel. You were required in the field, and I deprived myself of the support you give me here." Lee passed his test to support his superior's efforts; he far exceeded contemporary expectations as laid out by the greatest authorities of his age.

Those same theorists offered few useful suggestions concerning the discharge of the second obligation of command: to adopt practices designed to help oneself succeed. Moreover, their few observations seem entirely unsuited to Robert E. Lee. Military theorists tended to view generalship as a young man's endeavor. A senior commander, wrote one French general, required great bodily strength as "proof against the greatest fatigue." Indeed, he should be "called to the chief command at an early age" while still enjoying "wonderful energy." As a man in his mid-50s, Lee was successful despite his cardiac episodes and related health issues, and this put him at odds with the widely accepted views of his times.

It is difficult, too, to see Lee adhering to that French general's prescription to adopt "a mode of living . . . as magnificent as his fortune may permit" or to take pride in a headquarters designed for "the exercise of the greatest hospitality." Lee routinely sent gifts of food to the hospitals and dined on such delicacies as boiled cabbage. He preferred his tent to a house, however willingly offered. However, he did possess what most authors considered to be the ideal demeanor for a general, especially when in the presence of subordinates. An outstanding general, one author argued, must demonstrate a "bearing characterized by calmness," but without eliminating entirely "that dash and impetuosity so well calculated to inspire and carry with it those who witness the same." "Lee to the rear" episodes—so different from his usual outward demonstrations of calm—proved his capacity for this. Indeed, Lee usually proved successful in compartmentalizing his emotions, giving an appearance of steadiness even when wracked by personal anguish, as when his daughter died in 1862.

Lee placed service over self, sometimes so much so that he did not apply his best professional knowledge to implement sensible organizational changes that would improve efficiency. Notably, Lee never enjoyed staff support sufficient for a force the size of the Army of Northern Virginia. Nor did his staff officers generally hold rank commensurate with their responsibilities. When a Louisiana senator introduced legislation in 1863 to improve the quality of staff work, Lee's letter of support to Davis revealed a deep understanding of contemporary professional thought on staff organization and the qualifications and authority of staff officers, but he rarely applied his well-considered views to his own staff. For most of the war, he made do with a handful of field-grade "military secretaries" to handle paperwork and a small cadre of field-grade

Robert E. Lee. Richmond, Virginia, 1865. Photographer Mathew B. Brady. National Archives and Records Administration.

"general staff" officers to carry out logistical duties. As one authority asserted, a good general may "dispense with writing" in active operations, so that "his head and not his hand should be busy." But Lee never appointed a chief of staff with the wide authority to act in his name as called for by many military theorists of his era. He briefly contemplated naming his West Point-educated son Custis—already a general officer himself—as either his chief of staff or his chief engineer, but as he was concerned more about the appearance of nepotism than improved efficiency, he did not push for it.

Thus, Lee accepted a substantial degree of personal responsibility for certain staff duties. He engaged actively, almost obsessively, in matters relating to intelligence gathering and operational security. As Jomini had written, "How can any man say what he should do himself, if he is ignorant what his adversary is about?"

Lee regularly relied upon such traditional practices as scouring captured Northern newspapers, corroborating local items through cavalry reports or personal observation, and forwarding important snippets of information to Davis with his own opinions on their credibility. He repeatedly asked Davis and the secretary of war to use their influence to stop Richmond editors from printing news about Confederate troop movements, lest they reveal too much to Union commanders.

But Lee showed little willingness to adapt to change and even less confidence in newer methods. While the Army of Northern Virginia enjoyed a signal capability, Lee often identified signal detachments as overpopulated and underperforming when he needed to refill his ranks. While he used the telegraph frequently for routine messages, he strongly preferred not to send information on troop movements over the wires. Toward the end of the war, in both his own operations and his interaction with political superiors in Richmond, he openly admitted greater confidence in the security offered by a mounted courier than in the speed of a telegram that might be intercepted. With the exception of his fascination with railroads, he seldom adapted readily to new tools or practices that might help him make the most effective use of his mental energies in a time of uncertain physical health.

Rather, he focused his energies on his third obligation as a commander: setting up his subordinates for success. Throughout the war, Lee set higher expectations for his officers than for his enlisted men. When he took command of the Army of Northern Virginia in June 1862, he evaluated the capacities of all his division commanders, got rid of some, and actively mentored his two most promising senior subordinates, Thomas "Stonewall" Jackson and James Longstreet. His success in that effort ultimately underpinned his command philosophy, which he defined simply as bringing his army to the right place at the right time, and then trusting to God and his senior subordinates to win great victories.

Lee took great pains to identify the strengths and weaknesses of all his generals, from corps to brigade command. He taught by example that officers must see and be seen by their soldiers. He held generals accountable for readiness at all times. He rode his lines often, and when he traversed a segment he deemed insufficiently prepared to receive an enemy assault, he immediately sought out the errant commander. When Lee found one such general relaxing in camp, unable to comment on the status of his defenses, the subordinate expected a tongue-lashing. Instead, Lee quietly complimented him on his fine mount. Then, with gentle tones but unmistakable authority, Lee opined just how much the horse would benefit from regular exercise riding the lines. Lee nearly always praised in public and corrected in private.

Despite such displays of kindness, Lee believed that strict discipline was essential to an army's success and expected his officers to instill it. "The greatest difficulty I find is in causing orders and regulations to be obeyed," he wrote in early 1863. This did not result from "a spirit of disobedience, but of ignorance." Although he constantly pushed his officers, he seldom felt satisfied with his brigade and regimental commanders' efforts to stop straggling on the march, to prevent unauthorized absences and desertions, or to enforce orders against depredations against friendly and enemy noncombatants. Even as late as August 1864, he struggled to find effective methods to compel officers to enforce discipline, even if it "necessarily confines them to their duties, their camp & mess," and "deprives them of pleasant visits, dinners &c."

Lee thought well of the professional proficiency of the officers of his artillery batteries and battalions, but he worried considerably about the leadership qualities of the officers of his cavalry regiments. He believed that the commander must set the tone, and until the end of the war, he encouraged the best effort from his officers and exerted his influence with Davis and the secretary of war to promote and assign brigade and even regimental commanders who would be accountable for the discipline of their troops.

Thus, Lee was very much an "officer's general," but the enduring image of Lee as a "soldier's general" is impossible to ignore. Unlike the armies of mercenaries, conscripts, and disenfranchised soldiers who served in the European armies most military theorists of Lee's era wrote about, Lee himself never forgot he commanded a force of citizen soldiers. Even though he opposed the practice in principle, he appreciated that a Georgian had to be assigned command of a leaderless Georgia brigade because "it may be more agreeable to the men," a consideration, he wrote, that carries "much weight with me." He shared their hardships. He understood that positive reward had a place alongside strict discipline. To reduce the desertion rate, he instituted a system of meritorious furloughs to encourage good service with a highly desirable reward, but he still supported execution of deserters if circumstances demanded it. He made time for soldiers to attend religious services. He became the soldiers' advocate to address their needs, large and small; in a letter to Davis in the summer of 1864, he related a shortage of soap to soldier morale and self-respect, in the process linking a seemingly insignificant personal need to operational success.

Comparisons of the Civil War's senior military leaders often cast Lee as a traditional—even old-fashioned—commander and Grant as a modern general. Perhaps that conclusion requires reconsideration. With no real guidance from the best military authorities of his era, Lee quickly came to understand the interrelatedness of political, social, economic, diplomatic, and military matters and advised his superiors frankly and practically on the most effective ways—and not only military ways—to apply the limited resources available to achieving the Confederacy's primary objective: independence. Indeed, Lee's embrace of all the elements of national power foreshadows the way in which today's military officers attending the various American war colleges learn to think about national security strategy. Lee's ability to think about "big picture" matters well beyond those directly concerning his Army of Northern Virginia consistently demonstrated a breadth of strategic acumen far exceeding that expected of professional soldiers of his generation. These observations do not support the notion of Lee as an old-fashioned general.

Similarly, in his dealings with subordinates, Lee followed his own inclinations rather than adhere to the ideas prevailing in his era. Most military writers of Lee's time portrayed armies as machines in which individual soldiers existed as faceless cogs. But Lee kept in mind the essential humanity of the men and boys who followed him. Lee understood and acted early upon a lesson that many of his contemporaries learned slowly or did not learn at all: a link existed between taking care of individual soldiers and the success of the army and the larger strategic objectives they served.

As a general and a leader, Lee exceeded the expectations of his time to help his superiors succeed. He certainly viewed his relationship with his men a bit differently than did the military authorities of his era. Only in the second test—what he did to support his own efforts—does he fall short of the practices advocated by the military classics of his day. He did not appreciate that a leader's awareness of his own talents, tools, and limitations must remain the constant companion of even the most dedicated selfless servant. Nonetheless, Lee has many substantive lessons to teach modern generations about leadership, especially when we take him on his own terms.

Ulysses S. Grant. 1865. Photographer Frederick Gutekunst. Library of Congress Prints and Photographs Division.

# WHAT WAS GRANT LIKE?

JOSIAH BUNTING

Earlier today, in a presentation on Robert E. Lee, a scholar described the willing subordination by a subordinate to orders with which the subordinate might disagree. A memorable Virginia Military Institute story reinforces the point about leadership: In 1920, George Marshall returned to the U.S. as an aide to John Pershing. Brigadier General Francis Mallory, a member of the VMI faculty, asked Marshall what he had learned from serving under Pershing in the first U.S. Army in France and then as his aide. Marshall replied that the most important thing he had learned was the following:

> When you are given an order about which you harbor doubts, or with which you disagree, you must call yourself to account to execute that order with redouble the efficiency and visible enthusiasm. Those responsible to you will judge the order by how you take it and execute it.

When young officers hear that story, they tend to remember it, as I did.

Two weeks ago, in a seminar, a student asked me whether the world would ever again see generals like Lee or Grant, or like Eisenhower, Patton, Stillwell, or MacArthur? Have the circumstances and conditions of war changed so much that battlefield leadership of their kind is impossible, irrelevant, or unnecessary? No one in my seminar could furnish the name of such an American general now serving who was not named David

Petraeus. Petraeus, as I reminded the students, retired last year.

In 1940, Henry Stimson, the American secretary of war, congratulated the head of the Army on having selected what he called "good war men" on his first list of new generals to be sent up to Congress. These good war men had two main characteristics in common. First, they were battlefield commanders of large formations, mainly infantry. Second, many of them had blots on their records during peacetime service; they were men of eccentric career patterns and occasional lapses in judgment. Three of the five most famous American generals of the last big war, World War II, would not advance today beyond the grade of major. Battlefield command by general officers is no longer a matter of demonstrating physical bravery and grace and inspirational qualities under terrible pressure. Leadership has come to mean something else altogether—fiercely independent judgment—which tends to foreclose in the preparatory phase.

It took seven weeks for the admiralty in London to learn of Nelson's victory at the Nile in 1798. Today it takes less than seven seconds for Wolf Blitzer or Rachel Maddow and their millions of viewers to learn that a GI accidentally burned holy books or that a deranged soldier executed 16 people on whose behalf the government says we are fighting. Still, the subject of military history and the history of war retains a powerful allure for the lay public. Note, for example, the success of recent books on the subjects within its ambit: histories, biographies, and books of reminiscences. The subject broadly conceived, however, is ignored in the American university, where military history occupies a caste as low as home economics and whose practitioners are assumed to be either weird or arch-conservative or both. The reasons for this are plain and powerful. In the words of A.E. Housman, "The troubles of our proud and angry dust are from eternity and shall not fail."

We read and study and write military history for the satisfaction we find in a disciplined attempt to reconstruct an important part of our past and to understand what leaders of armies were like. Aside from leading a democracy at war—we think of Lincoln, Churchill, and Franklin Roosevelt—there can be few challenges to the human mind and character greater than leading an army or navy in wartime.

In the stories of how the leaders have conducted themselves, in the roaring flux of battles and the making of strategy, we find enduring and valuable lessons. The two generations of American civil and military leaders that represent the nation's very best, those who led and served from 1770 until 1800 and from 1940 until 1950, will repay study by succeeding generations, those schooled not only to learn but to use to advantage the lessons their lives have left us. One observer wrote of George C. Marshall, the great 20th century American secretary of state, "It is what Marshall was, and not what he did, that lingers in the mind." If we still believe in the guiding principle of education at the time of our country's founding, namely emulation, our knowledge of what we loosely call wartime leadership must form a staple of that education.

We are curious about the great generals. How were they raised? What were they like as children? What did they read? Who taught them? What influences quickened and molded their character? And of those we admire the most, those who are obedient to the strictures of conscience, we wonder, what made them that way?

When I began looking hard at the character of Ulysses S. Grant, I read everything I could get my hands on about Grant and the Civil War. My cicerone in this endeavor was John Simon, a singular man and a great Grant scholar in Carbondale, Illinois. Simon advised me to spend some time where Grant grew up in southwestern Ohio, a slow moving, quiet, conservative part of the country. I went to the battlefields and talked with other writers, including Bud Robertson, about Grant. I did my tour in Galena. Through all of this, I found that I was disappointed in my subject's shyness, his diffidence, his unwillingness to give voice to his thoughts. A biographer of Czech composer Antonin Dvorak pointed out that those who refuse to talk and write about themselves are condemned to be written about by others.

According to Mark Twain, the writer of an autobiography will "tell the truth in spite of himself, for his facts and his fictions will work loyally together for the protection of the reader." Twain attributes this idea to a conversation he had with another American secretary of state, John Hay. Hold on to that idea, because it also applies to the memoirs of Ulysses S. Grant.

From the beginning, Grant was what sociologist David Riesman calls a profoundly inner-directed person: calm, quiet, always keeping his own counsel, and bruised as a boy by others in the neighborhood who invariably called him useless. He was an average student, and the cliché so familiar to readers of military biography, which occurs about halfway through chapter two of the biography of every American general, also applies to Grant: "He was a mediocre student at West Point." Just before his last year, Grant was promoted to the grade of cadet sergeant, but as he noted in his memoirs, it "was too much for me," and he fell back into the ranks of cadet privates. Like many cadets, he did not work hard, but in an interesting aside in his memoir he noted, "I found myself reading novels." It was unusual to admit to having done such a thing in the 1840s. Grant clarified that he was not reading novels of the trashy sort, but works by James Fenimore Cooper, Bulwer-Lytton, and authors of that stamp.

Grant was regarded by his contemporaries as the great horseman of his generation. His introverted character was probably an asset in horsemanship, as was his size; when he arrived at West Point, he weighed just over a hundred pounds. He was a small man. In a famous photo taken near Cold Harbor, Grant appears as a thin, rather unprepossessing man who had just turned 42, stood five feet six inches tall, and weighed about 130 pounds.

Yet as a commander he had a quality that was difficult to describe or to measure, what psychologists call affect. He had an affect of quietude, calm, resolution, and determination. Making allowances for certain large differences in temperament, these are qualities also possessed by another West Point graduate, in a generation rich with men who became famous in the Civil War, Thomas "Stonewall" Jackson. These generals possessed certitude, determination, self-control, and self-restraint.

At the beginning of the Civil War, Congressman John Logan introduced Grant to his first Civil War command, the 21st volunteer regiment of Illinois, at the fairgrounds in Springfield. Logan, a famous orator, spoke to the soldiers for more than 30 minutes before introducing their new colonel. When he subsided he turned to Grant, who had only half of his uniform because he was still technically a civilian. Grant followed Logan's wonderful oration by looking at the fractious and difficult regiment and simply saying "Men, go to your quarters." The men instantly went to their quarters. If words were the coin of military exchange, none should be wasted. Language must be purposive and austere.

Some nine months later, Grant's response to his old friend and West Point contemporary, Simon Bolivar Buckner of Kentucky, was equally pointed and concise. Buckner was the Confederate general who was left holding the bag at Fort Donelson and who had sent to ask for terms from his old friend. Grant wrote back: "No terms except an unconditional and immediate surrender can be accepted. I propose to move immediately upon your works." Buckner sent a note back saying "I have received your unchivalrous note," but of course he was obliged to comply. Newspapers remarked that the initials "U.S." would thereafter stand for "unconditional surrender." It is poignant to remember that Buckner and Grant, like so many of that cohort of West Point cadets who became generals during the war, would remain close for the rest of their lives.

As an aside, it happens that the senior American general killed in the Second World War on Okinawa was a three-star general, Simon Bolivar Buckner, Jr., the son of this friend of General Grant. There are many connections between the Civil War and the Second World War. When the generation of Marshall and MacArthur, Eisenhower, Mark Clark, and so on, were still in their teens, they were taught by men who had fought at Gettysburg and Chancellorsville and Shiloh. The impress of the Civil War on that generation was very powerful.

In his memoirs, Grant remembers the evening of that first and terrible day at Shiloh, perhaps the most tragic of all the Civil War battles, was fought by gangs and groups in ragged cohorts of 18-year-olds from Wisconsin, Mississippi, Alabama, and Indiana. They were led by elected regimental colonels who in today's terms would be officers in the Kiwanis Club or insurance agents, quite literally. The leadership was untrained, and the resulting slaughter was unspeakable.

> I made my headquarters under a tree a few hundred yards back from the riverbank. The rain fell in torrents. My ankle was much swollen from the fall off my horse the previous Friday evening and the bruise was so painful I could get no sleep. I moved back to the log house under the bank, it had now been taken over as a hospital and all night wounded men were being brought in. The sight was more unendurable than the encounter with the enemies' fire or my pains or the rain.

Ulysses S. Grant. c1861. Photographer Mathew B. Brady. Library of Congress Prints and Photographs Division.

Sometime after midnight, Grant's friend William T. Sherman came looking for him, intending to offer the standard counsel of Civil War generals whose armies had been mauled and badly battered: "We should prepare to leave the field tomorrow." In his own memoirs Sherman remembered that as he approached Grant, who was sitting in the rain with his inevitable cigar, there was something about the general's posture, his affect, his expression, that moved Sherman to say instead: "We have had the devil's own time, haven't we, Grant?" And Grant answered quietly, "We will lick them tomorrow."

In virtually every one of Grant's battles from Shiloh forward there was a moment like that one, in which Grant, by his presence or by a word or two, somehow managed to inspirit an army that had lost confidence. Some months after the great victory at Vicksburg, in October 1863, a young officer named Horace Porter wrote a description of Grant. Porter, a uniformed civilian who would later be recognized for heroism with the Congressional Medal of Honor, was taken into Grant's temporary home, a simple house in Chattanooga converted to a headquarters. Grant had arrived after a 30-mile nighttime ride over the mountains in a cold rain. Porter entered the room and found Grant seated before a table with two other officers. Porter offered information about Union artillery emplacements and as he began to move out of the room, Grant said simply, "Sit still." Porter recalled:

> My attention was soon attracted to the manner in which he went to work at his correspondence. At this time, as throughout his later career, he wrote nearly all his documents with his own hand, and seldom dictated to any one even the most unimportant despatch. His work was performed swiftly and uninterruptedly, but without any marked display of nervous energy. His thoughts flowed as freely from his mind as the ink from his pen; he was never at a loss for an expression, and seldom interlined a word or made a material correction. He sat with his head bent low over the table, and when he had occasion to step to another table or desk to get a paper he wanted, he would glide rapidly across the room without straightening himself, and return to his seat with his body still bent over at about the same angle at which he had been sitting when he left his chair.... When he had completed the despatch, he gathered up the scattered sheets, read them over rapidly, and arranged them in their proper order. Turning to me after a time, he said, "Perhaps you might like to read what I am sending."

He was a functional man, efficient, utterly without pretense, dressed in the uniform of a private soldier with only the shoulder straps of a major general to distinguish his rank.

Within five months, Grant had been brought east by President Lincoln and given his commission as lieutenant general, the first in U.S. history since George Washington, and established as commander of all the Union armies, at that time aggregating close to 600,000. He elected to make his headquarters with the Army of the Potomac and initially stationed his headquarters in Culpeper, not far north of the Rapidan River.

His conversations with President Lincoln and what they disclosed of each man's notions of what needed to be done show a relationship between head of government and military command far better suited than the relationship between Jefferson Davis and Robert E. Lee. Each man sensed the other's confidence in him and their exchanges were easy and direct. Lincoln was capable of a kind of harmless disingenuousness when he wrote things to Grant such as "Your plans I neither know nor seek to know." He did not really mean it, and Grant, subordinate by nature, understood.

The Army of the Potomac would continue to be led by Grant's own subordinate George Meade, who was both touched and reassured by Grant's display of confidence in him. If Lincoln had expected him to "clean house," Grant did nothing of the kind.

The Army of the Potomac's Wilderness Campaign, according to Grant biographer William McFeely, was "a hideous disaster in every respect save one—it worked." It was the military strategy in the Wilderness, an affair of nightmarish inhumanity, that ranks it among the worst episodes in our national history of warfare. When soldiers of the next two generations were searching for comparisons to the agony of war in Argonne Forest in 1918 and in the Hürtgen Forest in the fall and winter of 1944 to 1945, they thought immediately of the Wilderness.

Americans are drawn to study the Civil War and the Second World War, and sometimes forget what the country went through in 1917 and 1918. Think about these numbers for a moment: in the seven weeks of the Battle in the Argonne, there were 26,500 killed and 110,000 wounded. Somehow that war tends to escape our attention and so also escapes the attention of our students.

John Wheeler Bennett, British historian of the German army who cherished a powerful affection for Virginia and also for the Confederacy and for the Civil War, remarked that there are two fundamental staples, intellect and character, of successful military generalship. The first is "military strategic genius" which we impute obviously and know that General Meade possessed in large measure. The second is what Wheeler Bennett called simply "the ability to rally an army in defeat." He meant something larger than that, something that communicated itself to an army: a confidence, faith, the certitude that the army would succeed.

Ulysses S. Grant did what he had to do. He understood the costs and he accepted them. I will never forget the story of the Union soldiers the night before Cold Harbor, who could foresee how bad the battle would be and so pinned to their uniforms pieces of paper on which were written their names and addresses so that their bodies could be identified after the battle. There is no more poignant testimonial to what we ask of 18- and 19-year-old people when we send them to war.

Grant was an imperturbable man. He had educated and trained himself to absorb and accept whatever his experience threw at him. He was a product of his own conscious manufacture and lifelong surveillance. This was a Victorian virtue, and it is not found much in the U.S. anymore. A young person, or an adolescent in the case of Grant, decided what he wanted to be—not what profession or possessions or prestige to pursue—but what he wanted to be like. General Lee and General Grant both embodied that Victorian virtue. Grant infused that spirit throughout his army, demonstrating that character and mind need not be considered as distinct qualities. Character penetrates intellectual acuity and vice versa, and the great generals all seem to have had that.

What was Grant like? In order to understand Ulysses S. Grant, to gain a real sense of what he was like, one must read his memoirs. The writing of the Grant memoirs has been an important story in itself over the last couple of years. Grant was destitute and dying of cancer, and he knew that his memoirs, if well done, would allow him to leave behind a sterling reputation and also provide for his family. Written in the last few months of his life and published by Mark Twain, Grant's *Personal Memoirs* received critical acclaim and sold very well. The work is candid and full of magnanimous and sometimes funny comments about old friends and adversaries. Some of the best have to do with Stonewall Jackson, of whom Grant said, "If he had been at West Point for five years instead of four he would have graduated at the head of his class." Grant admired Jackson and called him a fine officer, brilliant and brave, but went on to add something to this effect: "But of course, he never had to deal with me or Sherman."

Ulysses S. Grant. Cold Harbor, Virginia, 1864. Photographer Edgar Guy Fowx. Library of Congress Prints and Photographs Division.

# Grant on the Eve of the Wilderness Campaign

James I. Robertson, Jr.

In Washington, D.C., the third year of the Civil War began amid an atmosphere of uncertainty. Over time, Union victories in the West had inflicted an erosive dismemberment of the Confederate states beyond the Appalachian range. Yet in 1864 the war in the much more publicized Eastern Theater remained a stalemate.

The Army of the Potomac at the time was by no means in a defeated or submissive mood. Some 100,000 soldiers were wintering in the largest encampment of the war. With Brandy Station, Virginia, as headquarters, the military compound stretched over a 10-square-mile area marked by tree stumps, dead horses, and thousands of crows flying overhead. Yet victory at Gettysburg the previous July had given the Union army a heritage and a newfound enthusiasm. For the first time, soldiers were writing regimental histories. All of them were drilling hard, said one captain, "and they showed it. They were trim and hard as nails."

On the other hand, this army had been immobile for months along the north bank of the Rapidan River because of Robert E. Lee's brilliance as an engineer. Using high hills strongly laced with interlocking rifle pits and a network of artillery positions, Lee had made an impenetrable fortress that could not be attacked, or at least the general leading the Union army felt that way.

George G. Meade was the only ugly commander of the Army of the Potomac. Tall, skinny, heavy-bearded, hook-nosed, with an uncontrollable temper that caused officers to refer to him as "a damned old goggle-eyed snapping turtle," Meade was actually a better listener than talker. In the autumn of 1863, a New Yorker wrote his parents: "Nearly everyone in the army, from the highest to the lowest, have lost all confidence in General Meade as a fighting man, but all have the greatest confidence in his ability to keep us out of the way of the Rebels." The army's provost marshal put it more bluntly: "I cannot make out [Meade's] plans because he cannot make them out himself."

Thus at the start of 1864 the war was continuing with no turning point in sight. As usual, congressmen talked much and said little. But the year was critical. A presidential election loomed in November. Emancipation was still in its first steps. War weariness in the North might reject the Lincoln administration in favor of a negotiated peace. The very fate of the Union hung in the balance. As early as January, feelings were strong that someone outside politics might be a good presidential nominee. James Gordon Bennett of the New York Herald went so far as to assert: "The next President must be a military man."

No such figure of prominence existed in the Eastern armies, but out west was a general who had just gained spectacular achievements at Vicksburg and Chattanooga. His name was Ulysses S. Grant. President Abraham Lincoln was well aware of Grant's fighting prowess and his victories. Lincoln now wanted him in Washington, not as chief executive but as general-in-chief of all Union armies.

First, however, the president did a little background check. Lincoln observed: "When the presidential grub once gets into a man, it can gnaw deeply." Indeed, Joseph Hooker, Meade's predecessor, had once talked openly of the need for a military dictatorship. Lincoln's concern about Grant quickly vanished when he read a January letter in which Grant had stated flatly: "I am not a politician, never was and never hope to be. . . . Nothing could induce me to think of being a presidential candidate, particularly so long as there is a possibility of having Mr. Lincoln re-elected." With that, Lincoln ordered Grant east to the capital. He would be a lieutenant general, a rank held before only by the revered George Washington.

On Tuesday afternoon, March 8, 1864, Grant arrived in Washington from his Nashville headquarters. Accompanying him

George Gordon Meade. Cold Harbor, Virginia, 1864. National Archives and Records Administration.

were his 13-year-old son Fred and two staff officers. Through some mix-up, nobody met Grant's train, and he had to make his way to Willard's Hotel unescorted. The national capital with its crowds of ambitious and greedy men was repulsive to Grant. He himself hardly qualified as imposing.

The modern, popular view of Grant is of the quintessential American, the hero of the republic, the simple son of a tanner who entered West Point reluctantly, fought personal problems after being driven from the army, but found himself in a magnificent way and led the Northern forces to victory in the Civil War. In late winter 1864, however, Grant hardly looked the part of a supreme army commander.

Five feet eight inches tall, weighing 135 pounds, Grant struck one observer as "an ordinary, scrubby looking man with a slightly seedy look, as if he was out of office on half pay; he had no gait, no station, no manner." A Massachusetts officer thought Grant "mild, unobtrusive, inconspicuously dressed, modest and naturally silent." Many in that generation of army officers accustomed to Napoleonic postures regarded Grant as little more than a Uriah Heep in shoulder straps. Even a female visitor to the capital found "a peculiar aloofness" in Grant. In a crowd, she commented, he always seemed to be alone.

The registration clerk at Willard's Hotel that March 8 was not impressed when a travel-stained and rumpled officer appeared before him. The clerk offered a small room on the top floor. Grant nodded his head and signed the registration book: "U. S. Grant and Son, Galena, Ill." A flustered, now-fawning clerk reassigned Grant to the finest suite in the hotel as the quiet lobby changed into a beehive of talking and pointing. Shortly after settling into his room, the general received an invitation to meet with the president that evening.

Unknown to Grant, the Lincolns were having one of their usual weekly receptions at the White House. Reports circulated that Grant would be there, so the crowd was larger than usual. Around 9 p.m., Grant made the short walk from Willard's to the presidential mansion in expectation of a quiet conference with the commander-in-chief. The Lincolns were receiving guests one by one in the Blue Room when Grant arrived. The president, who towered over the general by eight inches, greeted him warmly. So much excitement followed that Secretary of State William Seward herded the crowd into the larger East Room.

Grant, a dignitary reported, "blushed like a school girl." His discomfort increased when Seward insisted that Grant stand on a sofa so that everyone could get a better look at him. A newspaperman wrote: "It was the only real mob I ever saw in the White House. For once the President of the United States was not the chief figure in the picture. The little, scared-looking man who stood on the crimson-colored sofa was the idol of the hour." When he at last escaped, Grant was "flushed, heated and perspiring with the unwonted exertion."

The next afternoon Grant met with Lincoln and the cabinet. The president officially announced the appointment as lieutenant general in charge of all Federal forces. Grant's response was a far cry from the bombastic pronouncements of earlier commanders George McClellan and Joseph Hooker. Grant thanked Lincoln for the high honor. "I feel the full weight of the responsibilities now devolving on me," he stated in a very short acknowledgement. "It will be my earnest endeavor not to disappoint your expectations."

Grant's stay in Washington was brief. He agreed to have a photograph taken, bowed out of an evening social affair planned in his honor, and headed south to get a first view of the Army of the Potomac. Grant was figuratively and literally alone when he arrived at army headquarters. No one knew him personally; he faced an officer corps of strangers more intrigued than inspired by the stern, unfamiliar figure now in charge.

New York Colonel Charles Wainwright thought Grant "stumpy, unmilitary, slouchy, Western-looking; very ordinary in fact." Meade's chief of staff considered Grant possessed of a "good deal of rough dignity," and he added: "He wears an expression as if he had determined to drive his head through a brick wall, and was about to do it."

One of Grant's uncertainties on that first visit was whether or not to keep Meade at the head of the army. The Pennsylvanian surprised Grant. He immediately volunteered to relinquish command without a murmur if Grant wished to put Sherman or another westerner in charge of the army. Meade added that he would gladly serve to the best of his ability in any post the general-in-chief desired.

That humble offering, Grant would later write, "gave me a more favorable opinion of Meade than did his great victory at Gettysburg." Meade would continue in his present position, Grant replied. Besides, Sherman could not be spared from the West. Meade would be treated as Grant intended to treat all other commanders: Grant would set the broad objectives of a campaign and stay away from "the minutiae of command."

Initially Meade grumbled that Grant might get all of the credit for any successes in the spring campaign. Yet Meade soon told his wife that he cheerfully would give Grant "all credit if he can bring the war to a close."

This statement deserves historical attention. Of the five commanders of the Army of the Potomac, only George Meade accepted second place and worked so devotedly in a subordinate position. It is inconceivable that Irvin McDowell, George McClellan, Ambrose Burnside, or Joseph Hooker would have willingly given the cooperation that Meade tendered for the remainder of the war. From their first meeting, Grant and Meade sensed that they could work well together. Mutual warmth and respect between the two officers was a major factor behind Union successes in Virginia that last year of the war.

In mid-March, Grant returned briefly to the West. He had by then made a number of decisions. It was impossible to command

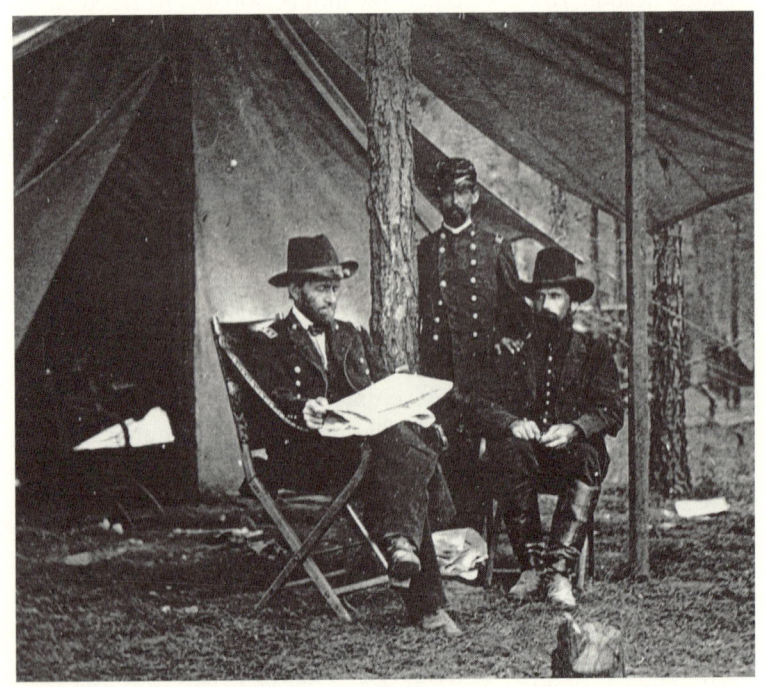

Ulysses S. Grant with Theodore S. Bowers and John A. Rawlins. Cold Harbor, Virginia, 1864. Library of Congress Prints and Photographs Division.

all of the Union military forces from west of the mountains or from the capital. Grant had been shocked when he first arrived in Washington to find a congressional investigative committee still conducting sessions on why Lee—eight months earlier—was not pursued with more vigor after Gettysburg. Grant's close friend, General "Cump" Sherman, told him: "For God's sake, and for your country's sake, come out of Washington!" (As for the members of Congress, Sherman wrote his brother, "I hope Grant will make it a death penalty for one to go south of the Potomac.")

Grant concluded early that he would travel with the Army of the Potomac. Not only would his presence shield it from meddlesome political intrusion from Washington; Grant also knew that Lincoln had not been pleased with Meade's cautious leadership. Meade was a solid and conscientious soldier, but neither he nor any of his predecessors had ever quite been able to make the army fight with a "killer instinct." Part of Grant's mission, therefore, was to instill western tenacity and daring into an army that had woefully lacked both so far in the struggle.

Negative reaction followed Grant's appointment as general-in-chief. His success had come in the West, where, the eastern elite believed, a general could win a reputation without doing much. General John Pope was lingering evidence of that axiom. In addition, Grant appeared to some critics to have stumbled his way to success.

He was a lucky amateur in his baptismal engagement at Belmont, Missouri. The navy had given him a much-publicized victory at Fort Henry. Confederate ineptitude overrode Grant's blunders at Fort Donelson and forfeited a victory. At Shiloh he was caught napping and came dangerously close to a crushing defeat. His losses at Holly Springs, Mississippi, in December 1862 were inexcusable. The first assault at Vicksburg was a costly mistake. His failure to pursue General Joseph Johnston's army after the fall of Vicksburg recalled Meade's inertia following Gettysburg.

The victories at Chattanooga might well have come more from Bragg's bungling than from Grant's strategy. Now he was facing the best the South had to offer: Robert E. Lee and the Army of Northern Virginia. This would be an entirely new ball game.

One officer who quickly dismissed such reasoning was Confederate General James Longstreet. "Old Pete" knew Grant well: he had been best man at his wedding. Longstreet warned those who would listen: "That man will fight us every day and every hour till the end of the war." As for Grant facing the already legendary Lee, the New York Times asked rhetorically:

> That is true enough. But do these people ever think that, if it be true Grant has never fought Lee, it is equally true that Lee has never met Grant?

By March 27, Grant had established his field headquarters at Culpeper. He was near but not with the Army of the Potomac—a decision of his choosing. His war aims in the forthcoming campaign were twofold, Grant announced: first, "to use the greatest number of troops practicable against the armed force of the enemy"; second, "to hammer continuously against the . . . enemy and his resources, until by mere attrition, if in no other way, there should be nothing left to him" but surrender.

In other words, Grant was going to strike everywhere at one time. He was convinced that in the past the various Federal armies had "acted independently and without concert, like a balky team [of mules], no two ever pulling together." This had allowed Confederates to shift troops from one point to another to meet the most pressing danger. That was no longer to be the case.

Sherman, in the West with two armies, would drive southeastward toward the Army of Tennessee and Atlanta. Another army under Nathaniel Banks would move out of New Orleans and advance on Mobile, Alabama. Meanwhile, the major Union war effort would come in Virginia. Grant's strategy there appeared complex but was relatively simple.

He was not going to conduct a water-based campaign such as McClellan's mismanaged affair two years earlier. Grant now had multiple targets in mind—all designed to destroy Lee's army before it could take cover in the sophisticated defenses of Richmond. Simultaneous offensives by several Federal armies would also prevent the Confederates from reinforcing one another at any threatened point. Since Lee could not counter a threat from every direction, Grant designed four offensive moves.

General Benjamin Butler and his Army of the James would come upriver from Norfolk toward Petersburg and the underbelly of the Confederate capital. A second force under General

Franz Sigel would destructively sweep southward through the Shenandoah Valley, then turn east toward the piedmont rail junction of Lynchburg. While this was occurring, a third Union column would advance from West Virginia through the mountains into southwestern Virginia and sever the Virginia and Tennessee Railroad, the Confederacy's only rail link with the West.

The Army of the Potomac would initiate the major offensive push. Grant told Meade: "Lee's army will be your objective point. Wherever Lee goes, there you will go also." Meade's army would hammer straight ahead, unrelentingly. At some point, Lee would be in the open and subject to attack from one or more of the invading forces.

Grant left no doubt that the Confederate army, not the Confederate capital, was to be the major target of the 1864 campaign. He left the internal operations of his armies to their commanders, but from start to end, he encouraged and supported aggressive action. Union forces would manifest active rather than reactive conduct.

With somewhere near half a million combat-ready troops, Grant would lead the largest host any American officer ever had. He would put every army he had on the move in simultaneous offensives that would exhaust the South's logistical capacity and conquer the two major Confederate armies still left in the field. Grant was not one to deliberate, unlike the ill-fated McClellan, who thought so long and hard about a campaign that it never got anywhere.

Rather, Grant was a man of action. He would devise and try something. If it failed, he would try something else. His intentions were always the same: to keep moving forward against the enemy. What Grant proposed was precisely what Lincoln had been urging on deaf ears for the past two years. Now, in Virginia, this was going to be a contest between the South's best general and most successful army against the North's best general and least successful army.

April 1864 became the greatest mobilization month of the war. At Grant's appointment to supreme command, Lincoln told him:

> The particulars of your plan I neither know, nor seek to know.
> . . . I wish not to obtrude any constraints or restraints upon you.

> ... If there is anything wanting which is in my power to give, do not fail to let me know it.

Grant took the president at his word. He genuinely believed that defensive duties could be performed effectively by armies on the advance rather than those sitting still, and issued orders accordingly. When he learned that some field officers were writing congressmen, cabinet members, and influential citizens to secure military gain of various sorts, Grant quickly invoked the guillotine. Henceforth, he announced, any officer who took military matters beyond military channels would be court-martialed.

Washington bureaucracy did not escape his attention. Grant discovered early that some logistical departments—quartermaster, commissary, and ordnance—considered themselves independent agencies and acted accordingly. Grant insisted that the general-in-chief would oversee all such activity. The matter went to Lincoln, who happily told Grant: "There is no one but myself that can interfere with your orders, and you can rest assured that I will not."

All soldiers on leave were ordered to return at once to their units. Grant drew unneeded men from every far-flung department. Excess cavalry troops were converted to infantry. When Grant directed that thousands of soldiers manning Washington's elaborate defenses report to the army in the field, Secretary of War Edwin Stanton objected strongly. Lincoln overruled his cabinet member:

> You and I, Mr. Stanton, have been trying to boss this job, and we have not succeeded very well with it.... I think we had better leave him alone to do as he pleases.

Grant sharply reduced the number of wagon trains so as not to impede the army's movements. Large stockpiles of supplies began lining depots in Washington and northern Virginia. Grant ordered a million rations shipped to the front, 100 rounds of ammunition for every soldier, and medical supplies to accommodate 12,000 wounded men. With Grant's approval, Secretary Stanton ceased all exchange of captured soldiers. Not only would this guarantee that Confederate forces would remain strapped; it also gave Union soldiers a stronger incentive to avoid being taken prisoner of war.

The often-criticized General Henry Halleck deserves overdue credit for many of these massive preparations. Halleck was one of the Union's most senior officers, but his military skills were extremely limited. George McClellan thought Halleck "the most hopelessly stupid of all men in high position."

When Grant took the reins as general-in-chief, Halleck agreeably stepped down from field service and became the Union's chief of staff. He proved excellent at military housekeeping. His office became the operations center for Grant's orders to all Union forces on duty. Most importantly, by shouldering all of the administrative matters associated with the army, Halleck freed Grant to give full attention to events in the field.

Grant made only one major change on the command level. General Philip Sheridan accompanied Grant from the West to take charge of Meade's poorly led cavalry. Sheridan was then 33 years old, five feet, six inches tall, and weighed only 115 pounds. He was an experienced infantry officer, yet "Little Phil" would rebuild the Army of the Potomac's mounted wing into an image of himself: cocky, hard-nosed, and ever-aggressive.

A command problem waiting for Grant when he came east was the presence of General Ambrose Burnside's 9th Corps. It was an independent force stationed nearby but with no connection to the main Union army. Further, Burnside outranked Meade in seniority. Grant stood between them as an intermediary in a cumbersome situation. That would change after the opening battle. Grant would assume control of all tactical decisions and relegate both Burnside and Meade to secondary roles.

The new commander worked tirelessly throughout April, although he gave few outward signs of strong activity. His 42nd birthday passed without fanfare. He was often seen whittling on a stick while puffing on one of two dozen cigars he smoked daily. A New England officer watched Grant closely for a time and declared: "He had a low, gentle, vibrant voice. . . . Not a hint of self-consciousness, impatience or restlessness, either of mind or body; on the contrary, [he was] the centre of a pervasive quiet which seemed to be conveyed to every one around him."

No parades or grand reviews occurred during the army buildup. Grant preferred to ride casually down the lines, looking intently into the faces of the soldiers who were going to be fighting for him—and giving the impression that it was more important for him to see the men than for them to see him. Their reaction was respect, not enthusiasm, and that was what Grant wanted.

Such was part of a subtle change in the national mood that April. Inside the officer corps, cavalryman Charles Francis Adams noted:

> The feeling about Grant is peculiar—a little jealousy, a little dislike, a little envy, a little want of confidence.... All, however, are willing to give him a full chance.... If he succeeds, the war is over.

Newspapers reflected the same feelings, sometimes with more intensity. The New York Times stated of the forthcoming movements: "In all probability they will be the decisive battles of the struggle." The New York Herald agreed.

> If, with General Grant at the head and the struggle as it now is, we cannot put the rebellion down in the coming summer, we can never put it down.... If we do not end it now, we never can.

Grant paid no heed to such editorializing. He viewed newspapermen and politicians with the same distaste. During the army buildup, an eager reporter asked Grant how long it would take him to get to Richmond. Grant stared at the man, then answered dryly: "I will agree to be there in four days—that is, if General Lee becomes a party to the agreement." Yet, Grant added, "the trip will undoubtedly be prolonged."

An Illinois surgeon recalled that at the beginning of May, "we looked upon this man ... with feelings approaching to awe and wonder as well as admiration, and heartily wished him God-speed in his efforts." At that same time, Grant wrote Lincoln: "I have been astonished at the readiness with which everything asked for has been yielded, without even an explanation being asked. Should my success be less than I desire and expect, the least I can say is, the fault is not with you."

In less than two months, an unpretentious Illinois soldier had brought long-sought direction to the Civil War in the East. Union armies would now move on a common timetable toward common objectives. With 121,000 men behind him, Grant was ready to confront an army half his size but splendidly led. The significant point about Grant's strategy was that once he started southward, the Federals would be the aggressors. Such an offensive would take

Grant's troops crossing Rapidan River. Germanna Ford, Virginia, 1864. Photographer Timothy H. O'Sullivan. Library of Congress Prints and Photographs Division.

all the initiative away from Lee. In that situation, a Southern army outnumbered as well as immobilized had little hope of success.

Billy Yanks were self-assured, refreshed in mind and body, with perhaps a deeper understanding of why they were heading again into battle. Grant told Halleck as the month drew to a close: "The Army of the Potomac is in a splendid condition and evidently feels like whipping some body; I feel much better with this command than I did before seeing it."

And what of Lincoln's feelings? The commander-in-chief termed Grant "the quietest little fellow you ever saw"; however, Lincoln told a friend, "Grant is the first general I've had! He's a general! . . . I'm glad to a find a man who can go ahead without me."

On Wednesday, May 4, 1864, Ulysses S. Grant led the Army of the Potomac across the Rapidan River. A member of the 15th New Jersey stated that as his regiment went over the crest of a small hill, the whole countryside was laced with dense, dark lines of men. They looked like long fences except that the light sparkled on polished rifle barrels and flags whipped defiantly in the springtime air. The sunset of the Confederacy was nigh.

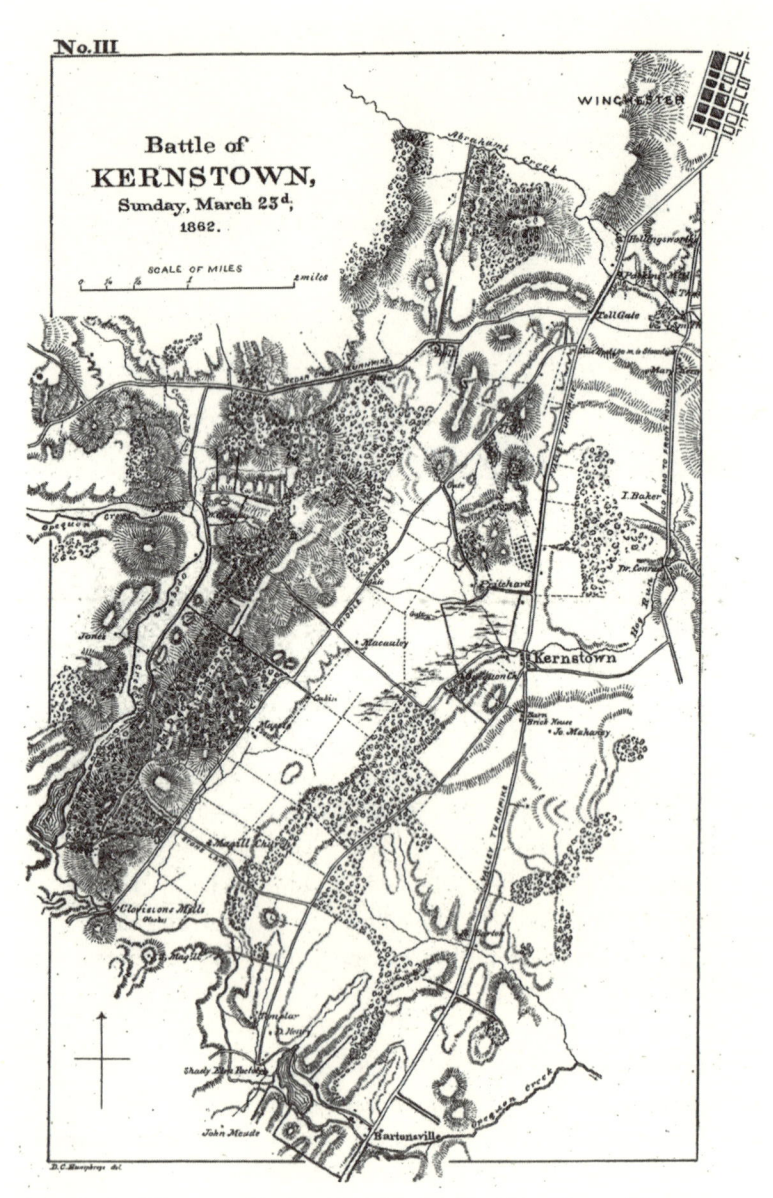

Map: Battle of Kernstown, Virginia, 1862. Jedediah Hotchkiss. Library of Congress Geography and Map Division.

# The 1862 Shenandoah Valley Campaign: Abraham Lincoln and the Union Defeat

Peter Cozzens

Secretary of War Edwin M. Stanton was not known for his sense of humor. But Major General John Pope got a rare taste of it when Stanton summoned him to Washington, D.C., in June 1862 to take command of the demoralized and scattered Union forces that Major General Thomas J. "Stonewall" Jackson had defeated just a few short weeks earlier in the Shenandoah Valley Campaign.

Pope said Stanton regaled him with a "comic account of the campaign" that spared neither himself nor President Lincoln. Stanton's remarks made it clear to Pope that the Shenandoah Valley debacle "was really a campaign conducted from Washington by the president and the secretary of war, in which the generals played no part except to obey orders. The generals," Pope concluded, "were entirely innocent of any responsibility for those operations."

Stanton never publicly confessed his or President Lincoln's role in the Union defeat, and history has chosen to blame the three generals who dangled from strings pulled in Washington: Major Generals Nathaniel Banks, John C. Fremont, and Irvin McDowell. While they all committed errors, the larger responsibility rests with Lincoln and Stanton.

Lincoln's first mistake stemmed from his frustration with Major General George B. McClellan. Lincoln gave McClellan permission to conduct his movement to the Virginia Peninsula in the spring of 1862 on the explicit condition that he leave Washington protected. In order to ease Lincoln's preoccupation with the capital,

McClellan promised to augment the city's 18,000-man garrison with 55,000 troops from the Army of the Potomac deployed in and about Washington.

But McClellan did not tell Lincoln that he had assigned the covering-force role principally to Nathaniel P. Banks' 5th Corps, then in the Shenandoah Valley at Winchester. Expecting no trouble from Jackson's small army, before McClellan embarked on the Peninsula Campaign he ordered Banks out of the Shenandoah Valley and into a blocking position near Manassas Junction.

Jackson upset McClellan's calculations when on March 23, 1862, at the Battle of Kernstown he attacked Banks' remaining division in the Valley as it prepared to leave. Jackson lost Kernstown, but the audacity of his attack suggested the Confederates were in greater strength in the Shenandoah Valley than McClellan had supposed. McClellan had to prevent the worst case scenario of a Confederate crossing of the Potomac River at Harpers Ferry and descent on Washington from the rear. Consequently, on April 1, McClellan directed Banks to reassemble his corps in the Valley, drive Jackson "well back," and then assume "such a position as to enable you to prevent his return."

Lincoln was also concerned about the safety of Washington. Examining the capital defenses more closely, he quickly realized that McClellan had hoodwinked him. Banks was 75 miles from Washington, and to make matters worse, in calculating the strength of the covering force, McClellan had double-counted one of Banks' brigades. "When the president became aware of this," Senator Charles Sumner remembered, "he was justly indignant."

On April 3, Lincoln clipped McClellan's wings. He countermanded McClellan's orders for Major General Irwin McDowell's 32,000-man corps at Fredericksburg to embark for the Peninsula and elevated McDowell to command a new Department of the Rappahannock with headquarters at Fredericksburg. McDowell would be answerable only to the president and the secretary of war and would assume the role in protecting Washington that McClellan had intended for Banks. Lincoln also made Banks independent of McClellan, creating for him the Department of the Shenandoah.

Lincoln was now the de facto general-in-chief, and he scolded McClellan:

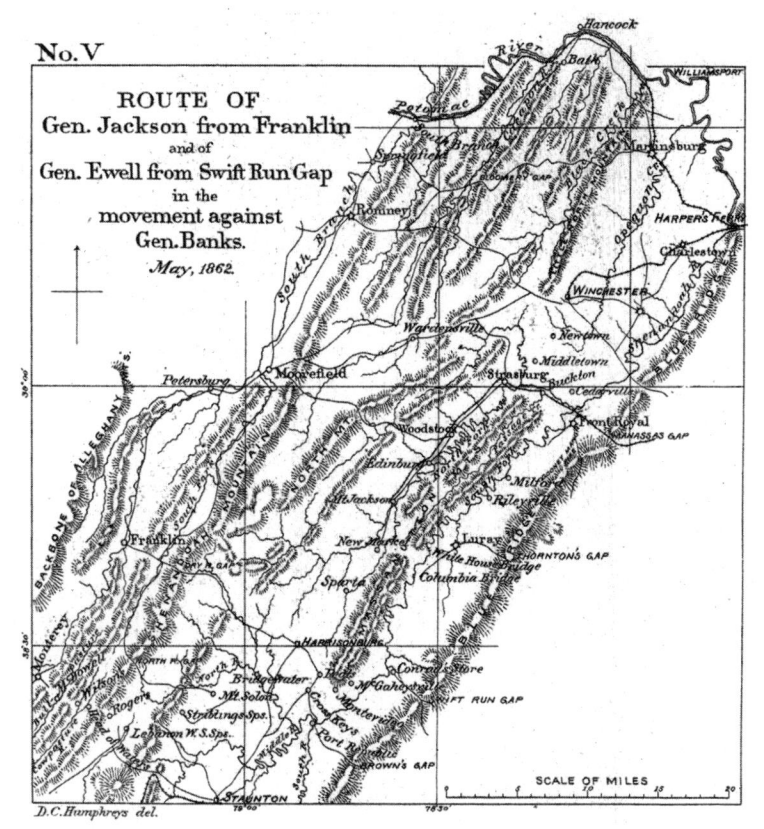

Map: Shenandoah Valley, Virginia. 1862. Jedediah Hotchkiss. Library of Congress Geography and Map Division.

I do not forget that I was satisfied with your arrangement to leave Banks at Manassas Junction; but when that arrangement was broken up and nothing substituted for it, of course I was not satisfied. I was constrained to substitute something for it myself.

This was Lincoln's second foray into the command structure in the Eastern Theater. He already had taken a direct hand in matters west of the Shenandoah Valley. To placate Radical Republicans, on March 11 he appointed their tarnished idol, former presidential candidate and famed explorer Major General John C. Fremont, to command the new Mountain Department in place of the immensely talented Major General William Starke Rosecrans.

In April 1862, there were three independent Union commands

between the Alleghenies and the Potomac River. Each reported directly to Washington. McClellan exercised authority over only that portion of the Army of the Potomac operating on the Peninsula. The president and secretary of war had taken on the mighty challenge of directing the specific movements of three widely separated forces.

The test of their ability to meet this challenge began in mid-May. Banks, who commanded the only Union force then in the Valley, was guarding the Union supply depot at Strasburg with one division under positive orders from Stanton. Banks had received intelligence that Jackson was heading up the Valley in strength. Because Strasburg could be easily outflanked, Banks requested permission to retreat to Winchester, a far more defensible position. Stanton not only denied his request, but also ordered him to detach part of his small command to defend Front Royal, vacated when Stanton summoned its garrison east of the Blue Ridge. Against his better judgment, Banks sent the 1st Maryland regiment, 900 strong, to Front Royal. That left him only 6,000 men at Strasburg to oppose Jackson's 16,000.

Banks' fears were vindicated when Jackson captured Front Royal on May 23, 1862. But Banks got no pleasure from being right; he was now forced to engage in a fighting foot race with Jackson for Winchester.

Here is where many historians have wrongly concluded that Lincoln and Stanton panicked out of concern for the safety of Washington. Stanton reacted to Jackson's offensive like the bullying but supremely efficient bureaucrat he was, and President Lincoln behaved as a captain of calculated risk, ever with a master politician's eye for opportunity in adversity.

But Lincoln made the wrong decision. He made what was arguably his greatest strategic error of the war. The crisis in the Valley was genuine. In the event Banks was defeated at Winchester, which seemed highly probable, Harpers Ferry and railroad communications with the West would be imperiled.

A complicating but generally overlooked factor that Lincoln had to consider was troubling correspondence by telegram from Brigadier General John Geary, who commanded a small force between Front Royal and Manassas. On the basis of information from runaway slaves, Geary reported that a huge Confederate command was bearing down on him east of the Blue Ridge. Until Jackson's strength could be ascertained and the Confederate threat east of the Valley confirmed, Lincoln could not rule out a Confederate dash on the Union capital.

The timing of Jackson's offensive could not have been worse for the Union. McClellan had at last concluded his plans for a final push against Richmond and General Joseph Johnston's Army of Northern Virginia. McDowell was about to move south against Richmond from Fredericksburg, while McClellan, who was only 10 miles from the Confederate capital, attacked from the east. Also, Fremont was preparing to carry out orders from Stanton to disrupt the Virginia and Tennessee Railroad, and then march against Richmond from the west. While there was no guarantee of victory on the Peninsula, the addition of McDowell's and Fremont's commands would give McClellan nearly three-to-one numerical superiority over the Army of Northern Virginia.

The question before Lincoln was clear: What should he do with Fremont and McDowell? Should he permit them to join McClellan, or should he employ them against Jackson and the unknown force supposedly confronting Geary? There was no panic in Lincoln's decisions; they were simply the wrong ones.

On the afternoon of May 24, Lincoln telegraphed McClellan his decision:

> In consequence of General Banks's critical position, I have been compelled to suspend General McDowell's movements to join you. The enemy are making a desperate push upon Harper's Ferry, and we are trying to throw Fremont's force and part of McDowell's in their rear.

Lincoln's orders to Fremont reflect his poor understanding of the logistical problems his field commanders faced. On May 24, he directed Fremont to "move against Jackson at Harrisonburg and operate against the enemy in such a way as to relieve Banks." Unbeknown to Lincoln, Fremont's army was near starvation and his cavalry was hindered by a lack of horses. A move toward Harrisonburg would take Fremont away from his base of supply.

Lincoln reacted to Fremont's explanation of his logistical problems with a rare burst of anger. Flustered, he referred to himself in the third person when he dictated to Stanton his response to

Fremont:

> You are therefore directed by the president to move against Jackson at Harrisonburg and operate against the enemy in such a way as to relieve Banks. This movement must be made immediately. You will acknowledge the receipt of this order and specify the hour it is received by you.

Lincoln dictated no harsher command during the war, or one so colored by ignorance of a Federal army's condition.

Relenting after Fremont's difficulties became manifest, Lincoln acceded to Fremont's request to enter the Shenandoah Valley west of Strasburg. Simultaneous with his unrealistic orders to Fremont, Lincoln directed McDowell to start for the Shenandoah Valley along the line of the Manassas Gap Railroad.

> Your object will be to capture the forces of Jackson and Ewell, either in cooperation with General Fremont or in case want of supplies or of transportation interferes with his movements, it is believed that the force with which you move will be sufficient to accomplish this object alone.

McDowell was devastated; he considered Lincoln's orders a "crushing blow," robbing McClellan of the chance to capture Richmond, destroy the Army of Northern Virginia, and end the war.

Jackson's defeat of Banks at Winchester on May 25 and subsequent advance to Harpers Ferry strengthened Lincoln's resolve to destroy Jackson's army. The situation augured well for Lincoln's plan: Banks had saved his small army; Geary's reports had been proven false; and Jackson's army appeared too tired to do much more than limp toward Harpers Ferry. Lincoln hoped to ensnare Jackson between Fremont, who was approaching Strasburg from the west, and McDowell, who was nearing Front Royal from the east, before Jackson could withdraw south along the Valley Pike. To McDowell, Lincoln said, "It is for you a question of legs. Put in all the speed you can. I have told Fremont as much and directed him to drive at them as fast as possible."

But Fremont and McDowell were unable to communicate with one another, and both Fremont and Brigadier General James Shields, commander of McDowell's lead division, were overly cautious. On June 2, Jackson slipped between their commands and retreated safely up the Valley.

The outcome in the Shenandoah Valley was secondary to Lincoln's greater strategic error. Simply put, when he ordered McDowell's 40,000 men to the Shenandoah Valley, he took his eye off the ball. The sole Union objective should have been the destruction of Johnston's army and the capture of Richmond. Had the principal Confederate army in the East been destroyed, Jackson's relatively small force in the Shenandoah Valley would have withered on the vine.

It cannot be argued definitively that McClellan would have captured Richmond and destroyed or at least severely crippled the Army of Northern Virginia even with McDowell's large corps at his disposal. But the absence of McDowell made McClellan more cautious than ever. Even with his habit of inflating enemy numbers, McClellan would have been hard-pressed to lose. The Confederates had only 60,000 men to oppose McClellan's 105,000-man army. To contest a simultaneous approach of McDowell's 40,000 men from the north and probable drive of Fremont's 12,000- to 15,000-man army from the west, General Johnston would have had to extend his already attenuated defenses to the breaking point.

When he spoke with John Pope at the end of June 1862, Secretary of War Stanton acknowledged the folly of the administration's decision to manage the Shenandoah Valley Campaign from Washington and divert McDowell from the operations against Richmond. But it was a recognition that came a month too late.

84 / *Leadership and Generalship in the Civil War*

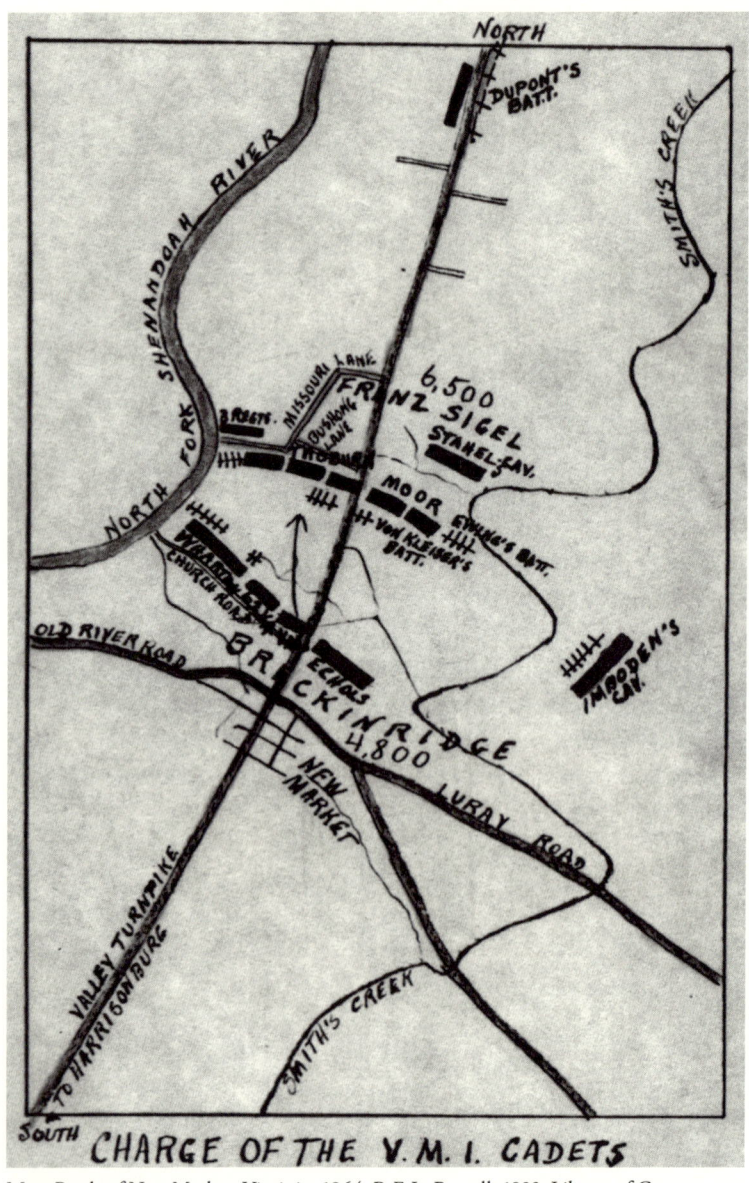

Map: Battle of New Market, Virginia, 1864. R.E.L. Russell, 1933. Library of Congress Geography and Map Division.

# The 1864 Shenandoah Valley Campaign: Military and Political Significance

Jeffry D. Wert

Thousands of campfires lit the darkness around Middletown, Virginia, on the night of October 19, 1864. Gathered around them were members of the Union Army of the Shenandoah. The day had been unlike any in their collective experience—a stunning morning defeat followed by a decisive afternoon victory. They were, in the words of their commander, "feeling very good." A veteran soldier of many engagements asserted that the day's battle at Cedar Creek "beats them all."

Farther south, up the Valley Pike, a different mood prevailed in the bivouac sites. For the officers and men of the Confederate Army of the Valley, a brilliantly executed surprise attack at dawn had ended in a headlong rout in the shadows of nightfall. "The state of things was distressing and mortifying beyond measure," admitted their commander. The outcome of the final struggle for the Shenandoah Valley was not "beyond measure." It had begun in the warmth of spring and had ended in the chill of autumn. In a bold gamble and against long odds, the Confederates suffered three major battlefield defeats and witnessed the destruction of the fertile region's farms, mills, crops, and livestock. Won during the crucial months of the northern presidential election campaign, the string of Union victories and the pillars of smoke marked the loss of the Valley, which was so strategically important to the Confederacy, and gave Abraham Lincoln's reelection prospects needed military successes at a crucial time.

The origins of the 1864 Shenandoah Valley Campaign began with a three-prong Union offensive in Virginia that started in May. Under the overall direction of General-in-Chief Ulysses S. Grant, Major General George G. Meade's Army of the Potomac crossed the Rapidan River in a confrontation with General Robert E. Lee's Army of Northern Virginia. A second Federal force commanded by Major General Benjamin F. Butler advanced south of the James River toward Richmond. In the Shenandoah Valley, Major General Franz Sigel's 9,000-man army marched south, up the Valley.

On May 15, Sigel's troops engaged Major General John C. Breckinridge's patchwork Confederate command. Breckinridge counted barely 5,300 officers and men in his ranks, including a battalion of Virginia Military Institute cadets. The fighting flowed back and forth for hours until a final Southern attack overran an enemy battery and broke through Sigel's infantry line. The Federals retreated, halting eventually north of Cedar Creek at Middletown.

Within weeks of the defeat at New Market, the war department in Washington, D.C. reorganized units in the Shenandoah Valley and replaced Sigel with Major General David Hunter, a native Virginian. Hunter resumed offensive operations, leading 20,000 officers and men south. They routed an understrength Confederate force at Piedmont on June 5, and then passed through Staunton and Lexington, wrecking rail tracks and burning warehouses and supply depots en route. By mid-June, the Federals approached the weakly defended vital railroad center of Lynchburg, where three lines intersected. To Confederate authorities in Richmond, Lynchburg and the railroads were too important to be lost to the enemy.

While the Union offensives transpired in the Shenandoah Valley, the two major armies in Virginia were locked in a series of engagements—Wilderness, Spotsylvania Court House, North Anna, and Cold Harbor—in the Overland Campaign. After the Army of the Potomac crossed the Rapidan River, Grant seized and maintained the strategic or operational initiative in the theater, forcing Lee and the Army of Northern Virginia on the defensive. The campaign shifted the conflict from the Rappahannock and Rapidan rivers to the Peninsula, east of the Confederate capital. Casualties mounted at a fearful rate.

Since Robert E. Lee had assumed command of the army on June 1, 1862, he had dictated, for the most part, the course of the war in the East. His aggressiveness and use of maneuver had defined the contours of campaigns. But then Grant wrested the initiative from Lee in a campaign that portended the eventual wearing away of Lee's vaunted army. If Lee were to regain the initiative and avoid prolonged stalemate, he had to take the risks of decisive action that had been a hallmark of his generalship for two years.

Lee decided to assail Hunter and resolved to send a force, as he informed President Jefferson Davis, "that would be adequate to accomplish that purpose effectively, and, if possible strike a decisive blow." He selected Lieutenant General Jubal A. Early and the 2nd Corps for the operation. In his instructions, Lee directed that if successful against Hunter, Early should march north, down the Shenandoah Valley, cross into Maryland, seizing military supplies, and threaten Washington and Baltimore. It was a daring endeavor that required the commitment of a fourth of the army's mobile infantry and two artillery battalions. Once underway, the audacious operation increased in importance, upsetting the strategic balance in Virginia for the summer and fall of 1864. It was to be Lee's final major gamble of the war.

Early's command raced west by forced marches and by rail and reached Lynchburg on June 17. Confronting veteran Confederate troops, Hunter withdrew into the Allegheny Mountains. With the Shenandoah Valley cleared of Federal units, Early marched north. By the first week of July, Confederates had crossed into Maryland. On July 9, they defeated a Union force in the Battle of Monocacy. Heat, a prolonged drought, and physical exhaustion slowed the Southern march toward Washington. Early tested the defenses of the Union capital before retreating back into Virginia.

A disjointed and feeble Federal pursuit ensued, but the Southerners eluded them, except for two minor rear guard clashes. When the main Union force countermarched away from the Valley, Early attacked another command on July 24 in the Second Battle of Kernstown. The Confederates routed their foes and cleared the Yankees from the northern end of the Valley. Keeping the initiative, Early dispatched two cavalry brigades to Chambersburg, Pennsylvania, where the raiders burned more than four hundred buildings and residences in retaliation for Hunter's destruction in the upper Valley.

Early's campaign achieved its objectives. It took the war to the edge of the Union capital, embarrassed the Lincoln administration at an untimely period, and forced Grant into a detachment of the infantry divisions of the 6th Corps from Petersburg to Washington. Writing about Early's raid into Maryland, the *New York Times* editorialized, "The thing seemed so much out of keeping with the position of affairs elsewhere," adding that it was "the old story again. The back door, by way of the Shenandoah Valley, has been left invitingly open."

It was indeed an "old story" as the newspaper stated. The Valley had been a region of Confederate successes, beginning with Stonewall Jackson's brilliant 1862 campaign. A year later, Lee's army used its network of roads during the march into Pennsylvania during the Gettysburg Campaign. Now, with military affairs elsewhere at a seemingly intractable impasse, a Confederate force had threatened the defenses of Washington, and 11 square blocks of a south central Pennsylvania community, Chambersburg, lay in ashes.

Lee understood that at this stage of the conflict the best chance for the attainment of Confederate independence rested in the electoral defeat of Lincoln in the fall. Early's operation had military and political implications. In fact, all of the major campaigns of 1864 unfolded against the backdrop of the U.S. presidential election. If the conflict appeared to be without an end, Lincoln faced defeat the polls.

On July 31, Lincoln and Grant met at Fort Monroe to address the recent events in the Shenandoah Valley. Grant had viewed the region as a subsidiary theater and had taken little interest in Early's advance into Maryland. He only slowly had come to appreciate the outcry in the North against the administration and its political implications for the president and the Republican Party. When he finally reacted to the threat, he dispatched the 6th Corps and redirected two divisions of the 19th Corps to Washington.

The conference between the two men resulted in the merger of four departments, embracing the capital, Maryland, Pennsylvania, and the Shenandoah Valley, into the Middle Military Division. The war department's response to the Confederate raid had been hampered by these multiple layers in the command bureaucracy.

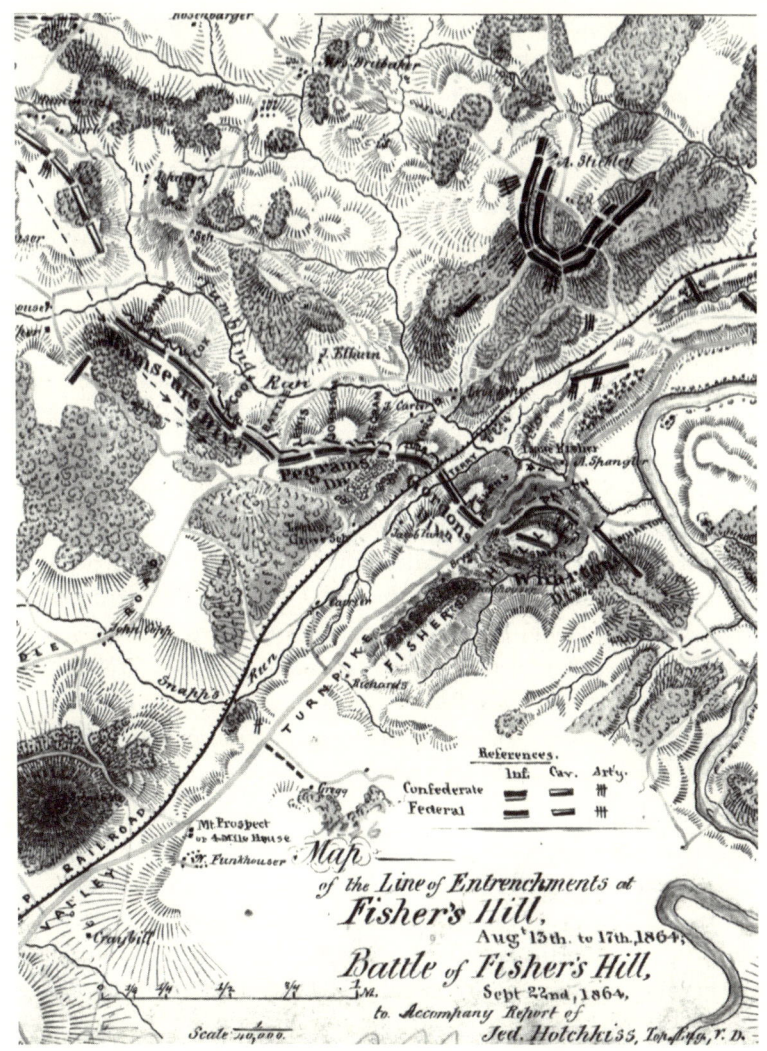

Map detail: Battle of Fisher's Hill, Virginia, 1864. Jedediah Hotchkiss. Library of Congress Geography and Map Division.

What Lincoln and Grant could not resolve at the time was who would command the consolidated department. Lincoln left the decision with Grant.

The next morning, August 1, Grant informed the war department that he was sending Major General Philip H. Sheridan, cavalry commander of the Army of the Potomac, to assume "temporary duty whilst the enemy is being expelled from the border." In the telegram, Grant directed: "I want Sheridan put in command of all the troops in the field, with instructions to put himself south of the enemy and follow him to the death. Wherever the enemy goes let our troops go also."

Grant had brought the 33-year-old Sheridan with him from the West, where the commander had witnessed Sheridan's aggressiveness at Missionary Ridge and more recently in command of the cavalry in the East. Known as "Little Phil" because of his height, Sheridan believed that an army existed to bring war to an opponent. He was undoubtedly the type of leader Grant wanted in the strategic region. Sheridan left Petersburg for the new assignment on August 2, with his appointment officially announced five days later.

Meanwhile, the majority of units that would comprise the Army of the Shenandoah had gathered at Harpers Ferry. It was an amalgam of commands specifically organized for a campaign against Early's Army of the Valley. The Union army consisted of the 6th Corps, two divisions of the 19th Corps, and the Army of West Virginia, David Hunter's former command. Within another week, a pair of veteran cavalry divisions from the Army of the Potomac arrived from Petersburg. In all, the force at Harpers Ferry would number roughly 50,000 officers and men, with nearly 40,000 available for field operations.

Sheridan joined his new command on August 6, and four days later started it south against Early's 15,000 troops. When he had passed through Washington, officials at the war department instructed him to act cautiously as Lincoln's presidential reelection campaign could ill-afford another battlefield defeat in the Shenandoah Valley. Consequently, Sheridan acted with unusual restraint during the next six weeks.

The initial Federal movement halted south of Strasburg, opposite Fisher's Hill. Early's Confederates manned the fieldworks on the steep bluff. When Sheridan learned of the arrival of a Confederate force at Front Royal on his flank, he withdrew north, halting eventually at Halltown, a few miles outside of Harpers Ferry. During the retreat, Union cavalrymen began the burning of barns and mills, a harbinger of what awaited Valley residents.

The Confederate units at Front Royal had been dispatched by Lee from his lines at Petersburg. The decision by Lee to augment Early's force indicated the strategic importance he attached to operations in the Valley. Lee hoped that Early could achieve a major battlefield victory in the region that might further loosen Grant's death grip on Lee's army at Petersburg. For Lee, detachment of Early in mid-June had been a bold gamble, and now the Confederate commander raised the stakes, expecting more from his subordinate.

With the arrival of the reinforcements—Major General Joseph B. Kershaw's infantry division, Major General Fitzhugh Lee's cavalry division, and an artillery battalion—Early trailed the retiring enemy. For the next month, the opponents clashed at times in the lower Valley north of Winchester. Marches and countermarches, thrusts and parries characterized the operations, moving a Union officer to describe it as "a mimic war." By early September, Sheridan had shifted his army south toward Berryville, east of Winchester.

While the "mimic war" transpired in the Valley, Lincoln met with his cabinet on August 23. Reports from Republican leaders across the North had been pessimistic about the president's re-election unless the military stalemates in Virginia and in Georgia could be broken with victories. At the meeting Lincoln asked his department heads to sign, unread, a letter that he had prepared. "This morning, as for some days past, it seems exceedingly probable that this Administration will not be re-elected," it read. "Then it will be my duty to so co-operate with the President elect, as to save the Union between the election and the inauguration; as he will have secured his election on such ground that he can not possibly save it afterwards."

The Democratic Party met in Chicago, nominating former Union general George B. McClellan for president and adopting a peace platform. But within days, the war changed Lincoln's fortunes. Major General William T. Sherman's armies seized Atlanta's last railroad line and the Confederate defenders abandoned the city. On September 2, Sherman informed the war department, "Atlanta is ours, and fairly won." This accomplishment infused the election prospects of Lincoln and the Republican Party.

Sherman's capture of Atlanta moved Grant to bring a resolution to affairs in the Shenandoah Valley. The general-in-chief traveled to the region, conferring personally with Sheridan. When Sheridan outlined his plans for an offensive against Early, Grant

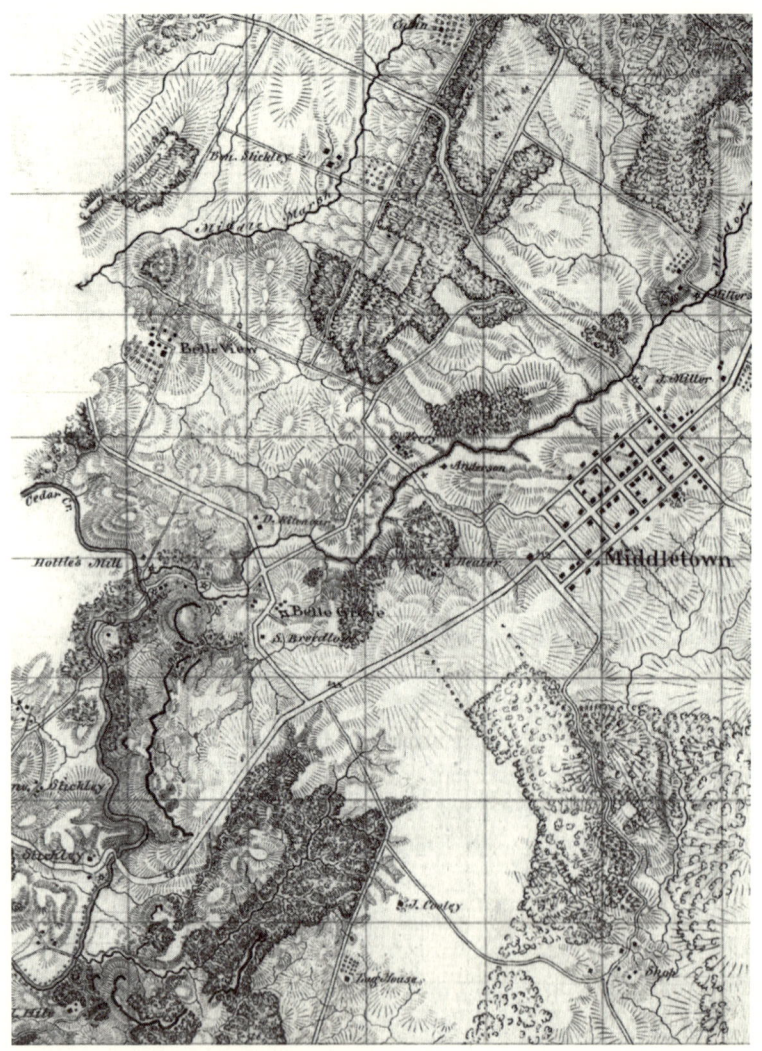

Map detail: Battle of Cedar Creek and Belle Grove, Virginia, 1864. Jedediah Hotchkiss. Library of Congress Geography and Map Division.

said, "Go in." Sheridan scheduled the movement for September 19. Before the Federals advanced, the army commander received a note, carried by a black man through the lines, from Rebecca Wright, a Quaker school teacher in Winchester. Wright disclosed that Kershaw's infantry division had been recalled to Petersburg and was on the march out of the Valley.

During the previous weeks Early had misjudged Sheridan's

cautious maneuvers as a lack of personal aggressiveness, even timidity, in his opponent. Since Sheridan's arrival, Early had conducted operations with consummate skill and audacity against his numerically superior foe. But the misreading of his opponent led Early to scatter his infantry divisions across the lower Valley. By nightfall of September 18, according to one of his officers, "Early had his troops stretched out and separated like a string of glass beads with a knot between each one."

The Yankees came on the designated day, advancing west toward Winchester. Only one of Early's infantry divisions confronted the Federals as they spilled out of Berryville Canyon on to the wooded farmland east of the town. Misunderstandings and miscommunication slowed Sheridan's deployment, giving Early valuable time to regroup his infantry and artillery. When the Northerners attacked at 11:40 AM, the combat became, in the words of a Confederate soldier, "a stand-up fight." The Southerners repulsed an initial assault and then hit a gap in the enemy lines with a counterattack, scattering Federal units. Sheridan ordered in a reserve division, and its troops closed the breach, driving back the Confederates. A lull ensued.

To the north, however, two Union cavalry divisions were moving inexorably, it seemed, toward Winchester. Early's understrength and ill-equipped mounted units opposed the Federals, but they were simply no match against the well-armed, well-mounted, and well-led Union horsemen. As his cavalry closed on Winchester, Sheridan ordered an infantry assault along his entire line. The Confederates resisted valiantly but were pushed back into their final line of works, shaped in an inverted L. The collapse came when the Federal cavalry stormed over the base of the L in a mounted charge. Early's ranks unraveled as his men fled south. One of Sheridan's men boasted that they had sent the Rebels "whirling through Winchester."

The Confederates retreated during the night of September 19–20 to Fisher's Hill, where they filed into the fieldworks. The Federals pursued the next day and deployed in front of the Confederate position. Unlike the earlier confrontation in August, this time Early's ranks were stretched dangerously thin. The Yankees attacked on September 22, striking the Southerners' left flank and front. Early's line collapsed and, once again, his men fled south in a stampede.

Fisher's Hill opened the upper Valley to Sheridan's army. The Confederates passed through Harrisonburg and then marched east into the shelter of the Blue Ridge Mountains. Sheridan halted the pursuit at Harrisonburg and, for the next two weeks, Union cavalrymen roamed the area, destroying crops, mills, and barns.

From Petersburg, Grant saw a strategic opportunity and urged, but did not order, Sheridan to cross the Blue Ridge, to seize the Virginia Central Railroad at Charlottesville, and to march on Richmond. Sheridan cited reasons against the movement and argued to countermarch his army down the Valley and to begin returning units to Petersburg. Grant acquiesced, but his instincts had been correct.

The Union retrograde movement began on October 6, and for three days blue-jacketed cavalrymen burned, blasted, and slaughtered nearly everything that could sustain Early's army between the Alleghenies and the Blue Ridge. The destruction was purposeful and systematic. "Clouds of smoke marked the passage of the Federal army," stated an officer. Valley residents called the three days "The Burning." Sheridan computed the devastation to be in the millions of dollars.

Early's army pursued, led by its cavalry units. A clash occurred between the mounted foes at Tom's Brook on October 9, ending in a rout of the Confederate horsemen. Sheridan halted his countermarch at Middletown, encamping the army in the surrounding fields north of Cedar Creek. The Yankees erected some fieldworks, but the halt was only a delay before elements of the army resumed their march to Petersburg. Sheridan departed for Washington and a meeting to determine the disposition of the bulk of his army.

The Confederate pursuit stopped south of Cedar Creek at Fisher's Hill. The bright prospects of August were faded, if not extinguished, since Third Winchester on September 19. Still, Lee wanted a decisive victory in the Valley. He returned Kershaw's infantry division to Early and advised the subordinate, "you had better move against him and endeavor to crush him." When a group of officers reported to Early that the Federals' left flank was vulnerable to an assault, he agreed to a risky offensive against the enemy. His army marched through the night of October 18-19.

In one of the war's most brilliantly executed surprise attacks, the Confederates struck at dawn. The Yankees fought valiantly, but the Rebels swept through the campsites, driving Sheridan's troops north and west of Middletown. By late morning, the offensive stalled from disorganization in Southern ranks and resistance from Union cavalrymen. Early and his army had won a signal victory, but their foes had regrouped on a wooded ridge a mile north of the town.

Sheridan, meanwhile, had spent the previous night in Winchester on his return trip from Washington. When he heard the distant rumble of artillery, he rode to the battlefield, arriving before noon. He rejected the advice of subordinates to retreat and prepared for a counterattack. He rode along the length of his lines, inspiring the troops. At 4:00 p.m., the Federals advanced in a full-scale assault. Early's proud veterans resisted the onslaught but, when Union cavalrymen shattered the Confederate left flank in a mounted attack, the Southern ranks disintegrated in a panic-stricken flight. The Confederates' morning victory ended in an evening defeat.

The campfires that glowed around Middletown that night signaled the end of Confederate good fortunes in the Shenandoah Valley. What had begun as a bold enterprise by Lee to regain the strategic initiative in Virginia resulted in three decisive battlefield defeats and the destruction of the region's foodstuffs and livestock. More importantly, the drumroll of Union victories assured the reelection of Lincoln. It now became only a matter of time until Appomattox.

Thousands of civilians turned out to celebrate the accomplishments of the republic's citizen-soldiers. "Grand Review of the Armies, Washington, D.C., May 23, 1865." Engraving from a sketch by W. T. Crane. Frank Leslie's *Illustrated Weekly*.

# THE IMPORTANCE OF STUDYING CIVIL WAR MILITARY HISTORY

GARY W. GALLAGHER

On March 4, 1865, Abraham Lincoln delivered his Second Inaugural Address to a crowd that had gathered despite drenching rains earlier in the day. The president and his audience understood that Union victory almost certainly lay just ahead. As the fourth anniversary of the outbreak of war approached, two million men had shouldered muskets in United States armies. Casualties among these soldiers—dead, wounded, and taken prisoner—surpassed 800,000.

Lincoln left no doubt about the important role United States armies had played. "The progress of our arms, upon which all else chiefly depends, is as well known to the public as to myself," he said in language revealing the direct link between military campaigns and civilian morale, "and it is, I trust, reasonably satisfactory and encouraging to all."

In a message to the Confederate Congress in May 1864, Jefferson Davis similarly had referred to the ties between the military and civilian spheres: "[T]he army which has borne the trials and dangers of the war; which has been subjected to privations and disappointments . . . has been the centre of cheerfulness and hope." As the conflict ground toward its conclusion in the spring of 1865, perhaps as many as 900,000 Confederate men had served, of whom more than 650,000 had perished, been wounded, or sent to Union prison camps.

Both presidents would have joined the overwhelming majority

of their fellow citizens in affirming the centrality of military events during four years of internecine struggle. Generals and their civilian superiors had planned and executed operations that not only included many of the most famous battles in American history but also profoundly affected the political and social dimensions of the conflict. Study of those operations yields a twofold return. Most obviously, readers encounter a feast of dramatic incidents, memorable characters, and striking contrasts of skill and ineptitude, of gallantry and perfidy, of triumph and shattering defeat. They also discover that myriad connections between battlefront and home front make attention to military affairs essential to any serious attempt to comprehend the entire meaning of the war.

Great captains and their soldiers always have dominated popular understanding of the war. Beginning with those who read the Century Company's landmark Battles and Leaders of the Civil War series in the 1880s, generations of Americans have enjoyed gripping narratives about huge armies maneuvering against one another, their generals seeking a strategic advantage to place opponents at risk. Once engaged in combat, the officers and rank-and-file members of these armies ensured the lasting fame, or notoriety, of mundane places on the American landscape. They fought for control of the ghastly entrenchments at Spotsylvania's "Bloody Angle," shed their blood profligately in a cornfield at Antietam, introduced their societies to a new scale of slaughter near a backwoods Methodist church called Shiloh, and waged a desperate struggle along an unfinished railroad bed not far from a sluggish stream called Bull Run.

Celebrated commanders bestrode the military landscape, crafting moments of almost impossibly high drama. Ulysses S. Grant carried out a brilliant campaign of indirect aggression against Vicksburg, reducing that rebel stronghold overlooking the Mississippi River on July 4, 1863, despite reservations among many of his subordinates and his commander in chief. Far to the east at almost precisely the same time, Robert E. Lee watched his confident Army of Northern Virginia sustain a wrenching setback in the verdant Pennsylvania countryside near Gettysburg. And 14 months after those storied events, William Tecumseh Sherman, who owed his success almost entirely to Grant's reassuring influence, delivered a powerful body blow to the Confederacy when he captured Atlanta. Told and retold by memoirists, historians, and other writers since the Confederate surrender in the spring of 1865, this narrative of the war comes closer to serving as an American *Iliad* than any other part of our national past.

Although no equivalent of Homer emerged from the host of authors who wrote about the military history of the Civil War, a number of superb historians combined descriptive and analytical gifts in a way to influence huge audiences. Two of the best were Bruce Catton and Douglas Southall Freeman, who between them authored a number of classic titles between the mid-1930s and the mid-1960s that still have much to offer readers. Two passages illustrate why Catton and Freeman, and others who wrote well in a traditional narrative style, have won so many admirers. In *Glory Road*, published in 1952 as the second of three volumes in his Army of the Potomac Trilogy, Catton memorably brought the Iron Brigade, comprising five regiments from the Midwest, onto a field at Gettysburg where it would lose roughly two thirds of its 1,800 men in a few hours on July 1. Setting the stage for a bloody day's work, Catton writes:

> [T]he Westerners fell into step and came swinging up the road . . . their black hats tilted down over their eyes, rifle barrels sparkling in the morning sun. . . . On the ridge to the west there was a crackle of small-arms fire and a steady crashing of cannon, with a long soiled cloud of smoke drifting up in the still morning air, and at the head of the column the drums and the fifes were loud—playing "The Girl I left Behind Me," probably, that perennial theme song of the Army of the Potomac, playing the Iron Brigade into its last great fight.

Freeman combined battle narratives and biographical portraits in *Lee's Lieutenants: A Study in Command*, a trilogy about officers in the Confederacy's most important army that appeared between 1942 and 1944 and served as an impressive supplement to the author's Pulitzer Prize-winning biography of Lee. The son of a Confederate veteran, Freeman embraced some Lost Cause interpretive conventions—an anachronistic dimension of his books that modern readers should keep in mind. Yet his descriptive prose and character sketches remain engaging and informative, as when he dealt with artillery fighting on May 3, 1863, at Chancellorsville:

> At Hazel Grove, in short, the finest artillerists of the Army of Northern Virginia were having their greatest day. They had improved guns, better ammunition, and superior organization. Officers and men were conscious of this and of the destruction they were working. For once they were fighting on equal terms against an adversary who on fields unnumbered had enjoyed indisputable superiority in weapons and in ammunition. With the fire of battle shining through his spectacles, William Pegram rejoiced. "A glorious day, Colonel," he said to Porter Alexander, "a glorious day!" . . . [T]here might be much more of hard fighting and of costly assaults, but if those gray batteries could continue to sweep the field, the Federals must yield!

The extensive retrospective literature by participants also holds enormous value, though readers of this genre always must be alert for special pleading and efforts to settle old scores. The postwar writings of John Bell Hood, Joseph E. Johnston, George B. McClellan, and Abner Doubleday, though not without merit, typify work that reveals more about the authors' post-Appomattox frame of mind than about the events covered in the texts. Ulysses S. Grant and Edward Porter Alexander, in contrast, define the very best of reminiscences—beautifully and sometimes movingly written, deeply analytical, and often more perceptive than most modern historians.

The Union's greatest military hero filled his two-volume memoirs with a number of remarkable passages, few more instructive than his paean to the citizen-soldiers who saved the republic and killed the institution of slavery:

> The armies of Europe are machines: the men are brave and the officers capable; but the majority of the soldiers in most of the nations of Europe are taken from a class of people who . . . have very little interest in the contest in which they are called upon to take part. Our armies were composed of men who were able to read, men who knew what they were fighting for, and could not be induced to serve as soldiers, except in an emergency when the safety of the nation was involved, and so necessarily must have been more than equal to men who fought merely because they were brave and because they were thoroughly drilled and inured to hardships.

Without an appreciation of the fundamental importance of the idea of citizen-soldiers, it is impossible to understand the Civil War.

In this passage and others, Grant's memoirs help us, across the century and a quarter since they were written, grasp that essential fact.

A section of Alexander's recollections captured the feeling of community and attachment to nation among officers and soldiers that helped make the Army of Northern Virginia the Confederacy's most important national institution. On the morning of April 3, 1865, he sat astride his horse on the right bank of the James River opposite downtown Richmond. Lee's army was evacuating the capital, and Alexander, who commanded the artillery of Lieutenant General James Longstreet's 1st Corps, had just watched the last of his batteries cross the Mayo bridge:

> [W]e turned to take our last look at the old city for which we had fought so long & so hard. It was a sad, a terrible & a solemn sight. I don't know that any moment in the whole war impressed me more deeply with all its stern realities than this. The whole river front seemed to be in flames, amid which occasional heavy explosions were heard, & the black smoke spreading & hanging over the city seemed to be full of dreadful portents. I rode on with a distinctly heavy heart & with a peculiar sort of feeling of orphanage.

Critics of military history often question the need to examine what they dismiss as "drums and bugle" topics. People in the non-academic world likely would be surprised to learn that students can emerge from programs in American history at many good universities without any knowledge of the military side of the Civil War—indeed, can take courses devoted to the conflict that include almost no attention to generals, campaigns, and armies.

Such courses focus on the home fronts, on the ways in which the conflict affected or did not affect the daily rhythms of life on farms and in cities. Hotly contested political issues also stand out. For example, how and when would emancipation be accomplished? And who should get credit for removing the stain of slavery that had mocked the noble language of the founding generation? Would the Republicans enact their legislative program? And did their agenda anticipate the emergence, later in the century, of a capitalist behemoth gaining world power status in the 20th century?

In this version of the Civil War, yeoman farmers in the Confederacy grew disenchanted with a government that seemed to favor the wealthy, as did anthracite coal miners in Pennsylvania's northeastern regions. Women on both sides struggled to find their roles amid changing conceptions of what it meant to be a patriotic mother, and sometimes, battling economic hardship, those in the Confederacy took to the streets to demand food. This version offers a cacophonous jumble of advocates and victims, all of whom act out parts of a drama that is mostly devoid of the boom of cannons and the rattle of musketry.

The historical literature on the Civil War has evolved in a way that often conspires against anyone who would engage both its military and non-military dimensions—who would, more especially, strive to know how the two intersected and influenced one another. Too many non-academic historians care for little beyond generals and battles and soldiers in the ranks, while most academic historians nourish a resolutely dismissive attitude toward military history in general and Civil War campaign history in particular.

There are exceptions to this generalization about academics, as anyone who has read James M. McPherson's immensely influential *Battle Cry of Freedom* or George C. Rable's superb *Fredericksburg! Fredericksburg!*—to name two notable examples—knows very well. As Rable aptly explains, the "'old' military history dealt largely with leaders, dissecting strategy and tactics carefully, sometimes brilliantly." Academic scholars brought a focus on common soldiers and social themes, but "gaining a full understanding of a battle requires looking at both sides of the equation and mixing the elements."

Acrimonious debates about filmmaker Ken Burns's documentary *The Civil War* and about how best to interpret National Park Service battlefields exemplify the continuing divide between advocates of the two Civil Wars. In his contribution to a book of essays devoted to Burns's series, Leon F. Litwack, a prize-winning scholar of the black experience in 19th- and early-20th-century American history, voiced concerns common among academic historians:

> Two major war fronts co-existed during the Civil War . . . the clash of armies on the battlefields and the social convulsions at home. *The Civil War* stays mostly on the battlefield, virtually ignoring the other war, the conflict fought out on farms and plantations, in towns and cities throughout the South, even where no Union or Confederate soldiers appeared. . . . None of the "great battles," not even Antietam, Shiloh, or Gettysburg,

compare in sheer drama with the way in which the Civil War came to be transformed into a social revolution of such far-reaching proportions and consequences.

Geoffrey C. Ward, the non-academic historian who served as principal writer for the documentary, responded in another essay in the same volume with some passion, insisting that Burns had tried to insinuate as much non-military material as possible into the "complicated, head-long, largely military story we found ourselves trying to tell." Clearly stung by what he perceived as an unfair attack from Litwack and others, Ward commented that "some of the criticism in this volume seems needlessly shrill."

The wrangling over National Park Service battlefield sites involved interpretation for potentially millions of visitors and received attention from the national press. In the 1990s, the Park Service began moving toward interpretive plans that would supply more political and social context for the battles—a process in which I cheerfully participated as a historian from the academic side of the aisle.

Congressman Jesse L. Jackson Jr. of Illinois shifted the discussion onto a highly visible plane with a speech in 2000 at a National Park Service symposium in Washington, D.C. The Park Service, Jackson said, in language perfectly attuned to most academic thinking,

> does an outstanding job of documenting and describing the particular battle at any given site, but in the public displays and multimedia presentations, it does not always do a similar good job of documenting and describing the historical, social, economic, legal, cultural, and political forces and events that originally led to the war which eventually manifested themselves in specific battles.

Slavery's role, he added, was most conspicuously absent from Park Service interpretation.

Defenders of a purely military narrative at battlefields mounted a strong counterattack. A cover story in *U.S. News & World Report* quoted Jerry Russell, a preservationist and thoroughgoing opponent of changing traditional interpretive emphases: "People go to the battlefields to learn about the battle. They're not there to learn about the economy, or women, or about slavery."

Because most Americans receive their first introduction to the conflict through battles and generals, I believe military history affords the best way to bring the two wars together in a fashion likely to attract the broadest audience. A certain kind of military history, framed to explain how battles influenced the home fronts and how, in turn, politics and public opinion shaped the Union and Confederate war efforts, will be required to accomplish the task. Success will depend on wooing readers who begin with popular treatments of battles and campaigns, piquing their interest in the other war and providing a bridge that will carry them across the chasm between academic and non-academic history.

Work on both Civil Wars undoubtedly will continue. Publishers always will allocate significant attention to campaign and battle studies. Gettysburg surpasses all other such topics in popularity. A bibliography of that campaign published in 2004 listed more than 6,000 titles. Interest among university and commercial presses in biographies of major and minor figures also shows no sign of slackening. Between 1991 and 2003, ten biographies of William Tecumseh Sherman and Ulysses S. Grant appeared. If readers consult the more than 4,750 pages combined in these volumes—or happen to read the two men's memoirs—and miss the point that Grant and Sherman forged a winning command relationship, they may turn to the 480-page book titled *Grant and Sherman: The Friendship that Won the Civil War*, which reached bookstores in 2005.

The point is that authors drawn to either of the Civil Wars should be alert to connections between the two. Any examination of civilian morale, for example, should take into account military chronology because events on the battlefield heavily influenced how people on the home front viewed the conflict and its likely outcome. Those calculations, in turn, affected the degree to which civilians supported intrusive governmental actions such as conscription, impressment, and taxation. Similarly, campaign studies and biographies of generals, which have added wonderful new detail and corrections to the complicated military narrative, should never leave readers with a sense that martial events transpired in isolation. The contending sides were democratic republics, after all, which guaranteed links between politics and military affairs.

That linkage permeates the history of the war. For example,

## The Importance of Studying Civil War Military History / 105

apparent stalemates in Virginia and Georgia during the bloody summer of 1864 threatened Republican prospects in the fall elections, prompting Lincoln's pessimistic blind memorandum for his cabinet in late August that predicted defeat. Happily for Lincoln, his party, and all who hoped to make emancipation a condition of any peace settlement, Sherman and Philip H. Sheridan delivered victories at Atlanta and in the Shenandoah Valley that completely reversed the tide of public opinion about prospects for Union

Military campaigns profoundly influenced politics in the loyal states. Sherman's and Sheridan's armies won victories in 1864 that re-elected Lincoln and guaranteed emancipation as an outcome of Union victory. Harper's Weekly featured General Sheridan twice on covers during his Shenandoah Valley campaign, including this engraving in the wake of the battle of Fisher's Hill. *Harper's Weekly*, October 8, 1864.

victory.

Similarly, Lee's triumph in the Seven Days campaign in July 1862 reversed a downward spiral of Confederate morale that had gained momentum following a series of terrible defeats in the Western Theater and McClellan's near approach to Richmond between March and late May. Lee's ascension to command of the Army of Northern Virginia during that campaign must be reckoned one of the great turning points of the war not only for the revolution he would bring in Confederate expectations of victory but also because his skill probably lengthened the conflict by more than two years. This in turn made possible the addition of emancipation to Union as a condition for eventual peace.

Nothing better illustrates the need to place military and nonmilitary influences in conversation than the process of emancipation. This topic has provoked considerable debate among historians assessing the roles of Abraham Lincoln, the U.S. Congress, and the contrabands—enslaved African Americans who seized freedom by running away from farms and plantations to areas under Union control. The concept of "self-emancipation" has been at the center of much of this debate. Its advocates dispute the image of Lincoln as the "Great Emancipator," insisting that slaves themselves played the key role by going to Union lines in such numbers that they forced a reluctant president and Congress to address their status. Lincoln's supporters, while conceding that for many decades too little credit was given to black people, reply that presidential actions were essential to advancing the emancipation agenda.

The decisive role of military forces in the struggle for emancipation usually gets lost in this debate. Yet only when United States armies drew near did slaves have the option of making a dash for freedom. Self-emancipation by slaves in large numbers without the military component would have been unthinkable. Similarly, Lincoln's Emancipation Proclamation would have remained an empty threat to Confederate slaveholders in the absence of operations that brought ever-greater swaths of the Confederacy under Union military control. The United States army functioned as a revolutionary agent for freedom—even, ironically, under conservative officers such as William Tecumseh Sherman, who cared almost nothing about emancipation or black people yet made possible the liberation of scores of thousands of slaves during his campaigns in

Georgia and the Carolinas.

Robert Gould Shaw, who would command the 54th Massachusetts Infantry but was then a captain in the 2nd Massachusetts, got to the heart of the matter in a letter to his mother on September 25, 1862, just three days after Lincoln issued his preliminary proclamation:

> So the "Proclamation of Emancipation" has come at last, or rather, its forerunner. I suppose you are all very much excited about it. For my part, I can't see what *practical* good it can do now. Wherever our army has been, there remain no slaves, and the Proclamation will not set them free where we don't go.

The geography of emancipation absolutely confirms the correctness of Shaw's observation. Union armies arrived soonest and stayed longest in parts of northern Virginia and the Virginia Peninsula, the lower Mississippi River Valley, parts of Tennessee, and areas along the south Atlantic coast. Those are the regions of the Confederacy where slavery was most disrupted, where the largest number of contrabands made it to freedom, where United States Colored Troops were most heavily recruited. Where the Union army did not penetrate—Texas, the hinterlands of Alabama, and much of South Carolina, to name three examples—slavery remained largely intact though the enslaved people there desired freedom just as ardently as anywhere else.

Most white United States soldiers and loyal civilians eventually embraced emancipation not as a grand moral crusade but as a necessary military tool to defeat the Confederacy, restore the Union, punish the slaveholders, whom they blamed for bringing on the war, and remove a possible source of future sectional conflict. Lincoln recognized this and sought to emphasize Union as the war's crucial goal and emancipation as one means to achieve military victory. Through this line of argument, he could keep the largest segment of the loyal white population on board with a stupendous national effort that exacted a terrible human and material toll. In his final annual message to Congress, dated December 6, 1864, Lincoln put it bluntly: "In a great national crisis, like ours, unanimity of action among those seeking a common end is very desirable—almost indispensable," he observed. "In this case the common end is the maintenance of the Union." The emancipation of slaves, added the president, stood "among the means to secure that end."

The Confederate army could take away the freedom that its opponent had made possible. During the 1862 Maryland Campaign, Stonewall Jackson captured Harpers Ferry, where hundreds of contrabands had gathered after escaping from their owners. Many Confederates noted approvingly that Jackson's force had recovered escaped slaves and captured thousands of Union soldiers. A diarist near Paris, Virginia, cheerfully reported "quite a victory at Harper's Ferry yesterday—several thousand taken prisoner and several hundred contrabands." Anne S. Frobel, whose section of Fairfax County, Virginia, had been occupied by Federal troops for much of the war, seemed to derive special comfort from Jackson's seizure of large numbers of runaway slaves. "We have just heard of the recapture by the Confederates of Harper's ferry," she wrote on September 17, 1862, "with 12000 yankees, and immense quantities of ordnance, ammunition, commissary stores and a large number of Contrabands, which in yankee parlance means negro."

On November 19, 1863, Abraham Lincoln stood on a hill that still bore the marks of raging combat. He looked out over a fresh burying ground and prophesied that the world would never forget what United States soldiers had accomplished at Gettysburg. That prediction proved true. But those soldiers should not be remembered only because they fought in the bloodiest and most famous battle of the war. They should be remembered as representative of all the citizen-soldiers who functioned at the absolute center point of the conflict, men whose actions and examples take us a long way toward grasping the origins, episodes, and meaning of the war.

All else did depend on the progress of the Union and Confederate armies, and we should use military history in a way that enables us, for example, to comprehend not only why George B. McClellan retreated from Richmond during the first week of July 1862 but also how that retreat shaped the political and social dimensions of two nations at war. Any study of the Civil War that slights the importance of military affairs can yield only the most flawed understanding of our greatest national trauma.

The Union army played a vital role in the process of emancipation. This photograph shows a group of enslaved people—some of them looking at nearby soldiers—crossing the Rappahannock River into Union lines during Maj. Gen. John Pope's Second Bull Run campaign of August 1862. Library of Congress Prints and Photographs Division.

Council of war: Ulysses S. Grant, George G. Meade, Charles A. Dana, and staff officers. Near Massaponax Church, Virginia, 1864. Photographer Timothy H. O'Sullivan. Library of Congress Prints and Photographs Division.

# Appendix: Leaders & Generals

## Edward Porter Alexander
### Confederate

Alexander participated in nearly every major campaign in the Eastern Theater, beginning as signal officer at the First Battle of Manassas (Bull Run). In the fall of 1861, he was transferred to the Army of Northern Virginia as acting artillery chief and later chief of ordnance. After establishing a reputation as a skilled and intelligent officer, he was promoted in 1862 to colonel and assigned an artillery battalion in General James Longstreet's 1st Corps.

Alexander played a vital role in the Battle of Gettysburg, particularly on July 3, 1863, when he was assigned to command the artillery barrage before Pickett's Charge. Alexander continued to serve with the 1st Corps during the Knoxville Campaign. He was promoted to brigadier general in February of 1864, and served through the Overland Campaign. During the Petersburg Campaign, he was wounded by a sharpshooter; he returned to command in time to supervise the defense of Richmond and the retreat to Appomattox.

## NATHANIEL P. BANKS
## UNION

Banks was appointed major general of the U.S. Volunteers by President Lincoln, who hoped to use Banks's extensive political connections as a former congressman and Massachusetts governor to gain support for the war. As one of the war's most prominent political generals, Banks tended to subordinate military affairs to political ambition. He devoted insufficient attention to tactical detail and was reluctant to admit or correct mistakes.

Banks was outmaneuvered by Stonewall Jackson while commander of the Department of the Shenandoah, especially on May 25, 1862, at the Battle of Winchester. He confronted Jackson again in Central Virginia at the Battle of Cedar Mountain on August 9, 1862. Banks was transferred to New Orleans, Louisiana, to command the Department of the Gulf.

In the spring of 1864, despite the misgivings of General Grant and Banks himself, Banks was assigned to lead troops in the Red River Campaign through Louisiana with the goal of capturing Mobile, Alabama. Banks's army started late, had trouble navigating the river, and was outmaneuvered and defeated. The aborted offensive was Banks's last field command. For the rest of the war he worked with Lincoln's administration lobbying Congress to support the president's plan for the reconstruction of Louisiana.

## JOHN C. BRECKINRIDGE
## CONFEDERATE

Breckinridge was elected vice president, on a ticket with James Buchanan, in 1856. Despite losing the presidency in the election of 1860, he was elected as U.S. senator from Kentucky, and served until October 1861, when he fled to the Confederacy. He became a Confederate brigadier general and was promoted to major general in 1862. Much of Breckinridge's service was in the Western ginia on April 9, 1865, and his stature as a general won him election as eighteenth U.S. president in 1868.

### DAVID HUNTER
### UNION

Shortly after the Union defeat at the Battle of New Market on May 15, 1864, Hunter replaced Franz Sigel as commander of the Army of the Shenandoah.

Hunter was notorious, early in the war, for disregarding Union policy and enlisting ex-slaves as soldiers without the permission of the war department.

He is best known, however, for "scorched earth" destruction waged in the Shenandoah Valley. On June 5, 1864, Hunter defeated Confederate forces at the Battle of Piedmont, and his army continued up the Valley to Lexington, burned Virginia Military Institute and the home of former Virginia Governor John Letcher, and looted private homes and the library of Washington College.

On June 19, 1864, Hunter's army was defeated by Confederates under Jubal Early at the Battle of Lynchburg. General Ulysses S. Grant ordered General Philip Sheridan to the Valley. Left with only administrative responsibilities for the Valley army, Hunter requested to be relieved of command. He did not command troops in battle for the remainder of the war.

### THOMAS J. "STONEWALL" JACKSON
### CONFEDERATE

Ubiquitously known as "Stonewall," Jackson was a West Point graduate, veteran of the Mexican War, and instructor at the Virginia Military Institute in Lexington, Virginia.

Jackson earned his famous nickname at the First Battle of Manassas (Bull Run) in 1861 when a fellow general was reported to have cried out, "There is Jackson standing like a stone wall. Let us determine to die here, and we will conquer. Rally behind the

Virginians!"

In the spring of 1862, Jackson was ordered to the Shenandoah Valley to prevent Union troops from reinforcing George McClellan's advance on the Confederate capital at Richmond. Though Jackson was repulsed by Union forces at Kernstown, he used speed and surprise to outmaneuver and defeat his enemies later, winning victories at Winchester on May 25, Cross Keys on June 8, and Port Republic on June 9, 1862. Jackson's campaign succeeded in diverting Union soldiers from the Richmond campaign at a critical moment and reinforced Lincoln's fear for the safety of the capital at Washington.

Ordered to reinforce Lee's army at Richmond, Jackson and his men were too exhausted to perform at their full ferocity. During this and in later campaigns at Manassas (Bull Run) and Fredericksburg, Jackson's subordinate officers found him to be demanding, inflexible, and secretive, sometimes to such a degree that it became difficult to carry out his orders.

After a successful surprise attack that rolled up the Union flank at Chancellorsville in 1863, Jackson was accidentally wounded by his own men. He died eight days later from complications of the injury.

### JOSEPH E. JOHNSTON
### CONFEDERATE

Johnston served in the Mexican War and as quartermaster general of the U.S. Army before the Civil War. He was the highest-ranking officer to resign his U.S. Army commission when the Civil War broke out, and he helped lead Confederates to victory at the First

Battle of Manassas (Bull Run) in July 1861. When Confederate President Jefferson Davis promoted him to the rank of full general, Johnston was outranked by three other officers, men to whom he had been a superior in the U.S. Army. Johnston remembered this slight throughout the war, and his feud with Davis negatively affected his wartime career.

Johnston was wounded at the Battle of Seven Pines on June 1, 1862, and Davis gave command of the Army of Northern Virginia to Robert E. Lee, who led it for the remainder of the war. In November 1862, Johnston was appointed to command the Confederate Department of the West. During his tenure, he and Davis quarreled over Confederate strategy to relieve Vicksburg.

In November 1863, Davis reluctantly named Johnston commander of the Army of Tennessee, and the following May, Union General William Tecumseh Sherman targeted Johnston's army. Johnston fell back into Georgia, sustaining casualties along the way, but inflicting heavy losses on Sherman's army. On July 17, 1864, as the armies approached Atlanta, Davis relieved Johnston of command. On April 26, 1865, after returning to the command of the Army of the Tennessee, Johnston surrendered that army to Sherman in North Carolina.

### ROBERT E. LEE
### CONFEDERATE

Lee led the Army of Northern Virginia from June 1862 until its surrender at Appomattox Court House on April 9, 1865. Descended from several of the first families of Virginia, Lee was an officer in the U.S. Army before the war; his decision to resign his commission and fight for the Confederacy was emblematic of the choice faced by many American people at the time.

Upon taking command of the Army of Northern Virginia in 1862, Lee repulsed General George B. McClellan's army from the Confederate capital during the Seven Days Battles and won victories at Second Manassas (Bull Run), Fredericksburg, and

Chancellorsville.

His attempts to bring the war north out of Virginia during the Maryland and Pennsylvania campaigns resulted in major contests at Antietam (Sharpsburg) and Gettysburg, with severe consequences for the Confederacy—not the least of which was the continuation of the fighting in Virginia.

Lee defended Virginia during the Overland Campaign against Ulysses S. Grant, but was outmaneuvered and forced into a prolonged campaign at Petersburg. When Lee's army abandoned Petersburg, Richmond fell, and Lee's army made its way south, planning to unite with Joseph E. Johnston's Army of the Tennessee. Instead, Lee was cornered at Appomattox Court House and surrendered his army to Grant on April 9, 1985.

Lee's generalship was characterized by bold tactical maneuvers, and as a leader he inspired his men. Since the war, critics have questioned his strategic judgment and his reluctance to fight in the Western Theater, concentrating instead on defending Virginia.

## Abraham Lincoln
## Union

Prior to becoming sixteenth president of the United States, Lincoln's military experience was limited to service in the Illinois militia during the Black Hawk War. He attained the rank of captain but never saw combat.

With the opening shots of civil war at Fort Sumter on April 12, 1861, Lincoln became a careful student of military tactics, and had to learn from experience. He came to stress two important strategic goals: ensuring the defense of the capital at Washington, D.C. and conducting an aggressive war against the Confederate armies.

Lincoln routinely disagreed with George B. McClellan, first commander of the Army of the Potomac, regarding the prosecution of the war and eventually relieved him of command. Lincoln's search for a commander to oppose Robert E. Lee eventually led him to Ulysses S. Grant, who took command of all Union forces in 1864.

As president, Lincoln exerted more executive authority than any previous U.S. president, declaring martial law in areas, drafting soldiers, and quelling draft riots with armed troops. His issuance of the Emancipation Proclamation on January 1, 1863 changed the Union war aims to include the end of slavery. Though his power to end slavery was limited by the Constitution, Lincoln declared slaves in the rebelling states free and effectively made emancipation a part of the Union war effort, as black soldiers were incorporated into the Union army. The war measure later became the law of the land through the ratification of the Thirteenth Amendment to the U.S. Constitution.

In 1864, Lincoln appointed Grant general-in-chief of all Union forces, displaying faith in his strategies, tactics, and ability to fight. That November, Lincoln won reelection with the support of Union soldiers, who voted from the field for the first time in U.S. history. General William T. Sherman had captured Atlanta two months before the election.

On April 14, 1865, Lincoln was shot by John Wilkes Booth at Ford's Theater in Washington, D.C. He died the next morning, only days after the surrender of the Confederacy's principal army at Appomattox Court House.

## JAMES LONGSTREET
## CONFEDERATE

Longstreet resigned his U.S. Army commission at the outbreak of the Civil War and entered Confederate service as a brigadier general. During the war he rose to the rank of lieutenant general and served as Robert E. Lee's second-in-command throughout much of the war. Longstreet served dependably in all of the Army of Northern Virginia's major engagements during 1862 and 1863 except Chancellorsville, at which time he led two divisions on a foraging expedition in southeastern

Virginia that included a short siege of Suffolk, Virginia. Even though Longstreet opposed Lee's plans at Gettysburg in July 1863, he dutifully executed the commanding general's orders and his corps bore much of the fighting on July 2 and 3. After the war, Longstreet was blamed unfairly for the Confederate defeat at Gettysburg.

After Gettysburg, Longstreet led reinforcements to the Western Theater and contributed to Confederate victory at Chickamauga in September 1863. He performed poorly as subordinate to General Braxton Bragg during the Chattanooga Campaign, and failed to capture Knoxville, Tennessee, during the fall and winter of 1863-1864.

Returning to Virginia in the spring of 1864, Longstreet was wounded by friendly fire at the Battle of the Wilderness. Longstreet returned to service in October to participate in the Petersburg Campaign and surrendered with the Army of Northern Virginia at Appomattox Court House in April 1865.

### GEORGE B. MCCLELLAN
### UNION

Called "Young Napoleon" by the press, McClellan enjoyed successes and suffered reverses on the battlefield that were accompanied by intense conflict with his military and civilian superiors, particularly Abraham Lincoln. After the First Battle of Manassas (Bull Run) in July 1861, McClellan organized, trained, and commanded the Army of the Potomac.

He maintained the respect of his soldiers despite the unsuccessful Peninsula Campaign and Seven Days Battles near Richmond in 1862. McClellan's unwillingness to engage his opponents aggressively characterized these campaigns as well as the Battle of Antietam (Sharpsburg) on September 17, 1862. Although McClellan forced Robert E. Lee to abandon his invasion of the North, he also failed to win a decisive victory.

After Antietam, Lincoln so was dissatisfied with McClellan's stubbornness and lack of aggression that he relieved him of command. McClellan ran as the Democratic candidate against Lincoln in the 1864 presidential election. He resigned his army commission on election day and lost the contest.

### GEORGE GORDON MEADE
### UNION

Soon after the Civil War began, Meade was made a brigadier general of Pennsylvania volunteers. By the end of the conflict, he rose to the rank of major general and commanded the Army of the Potomac.

Meade's most famous victory was in July of 1863 at Gettysburg, where he defeated Robert E. Lee and the Army of Northern Virginia after only three days in command. The victory was marred, however, by his failure to pursue Lee's retreating army aggressively after the battle. As a result, Lincoln began to be impatient with Meade's prudence and caution.

When Ulysses S. Grant became general-in-chief in 1864, Meade offered to resign or to accept reassignment to any command for which Grant thought Meade would be of most value. Grant declined Meade's offer, but when Grant elected to make his headquarters with the Army of the Potomac, Meade was relegated to nominal command of the army through the end of the war.

### WILLIAM NELSON PENDLETON
### CONFEDERATE

A West Point graduate and ordained Episcopal priest, Pendleton was serving as rector of the parish church in Lexington, Virginia, when the war began. He volunteered for military service and was elected captain of the Rockbridge Artillery. He eventually became chief of artillery for the Army of Northern Virginia but proved to be an ineffective commander.

At the Battle of Shepherdstown on September 19, 1862, despite a commanding position from which to defend the Potomac River crossings, Pendleton lost control of his forces and fled the field. In an exaggerated, frantic report, he announced that his position was lost and all his guns were captured; in fact he lost only four guns. He was accused of cowardice by soldiers and the Confederate public.

Despite lackluster battlefield performance, Pendleton was a smart administrator and successfully organized the artillery branch into an effective battalion system that allowed battery commanders to maximize limited firepower.

At the war's end, Pendleton and his forces surrendered with Lee at Appomattox Court House. Soon after, he returned to Lexington to serve as rector of the church Lee attended, which was later renamed and remains today the R. E. Lee Memorial Episcopal Church.

## JOHN POPE
## UNION

As a general, Pope had a reputation for outspokenness and arrogance. Animosity and indifference characterized his relationships with other generals, particularly George B. McClellan and Fitz-John Porter.

Pope served well in the Western Theater with the Army of the Mississippi in 1862, particularly at Island No. 10, and Corinth, Mississippi. His successes prompted President Lincoln to transfer him to the East to confront Lee and the Army of Northern Virginia.

Pope planned not only to defeat Confederate armies but to pursue a hard war campaign against Confederate civilians. This plan came to an abrupt end when Pope's troops confronted the Confederates at the Second Battle of Manassas (Bull Run) in August 1862 and were soundly defeated. Afterward, Pope blamed General Fitz-John Porter for the loss and had him cashiered for disobedience of orders that were later discovered to be based on Pope's ignorance of the situation at the time they were issued. Pope was transferred to the Department of the Northwest, where he was tasked with managing the aftermath of the 1862 Sioux Uprising. Toward the end of the Civil War, he served as commander of the Military Division of the Missouri.

## Philip Sheridan
### Union

Sheridan started as a staff officer for General Henry Halleck and rose quickly through the ranks of the Union army, ultimately being promoted to major general after the Battle of Stones River in 1863. After Ulysses S. Grant was promoted to general-in-chief of the Union armies in 1864, Grant made Sheridan commander of the Army of the Potomac's Cavalry Corps.

Sheridan took command of the Army of the Shenandoah in August of 1864 and in September of the same year defeated General Jubal Early's Confederate army at Winchester and again at Fisher's Hill. Sheridan and his cavalry then engaged in what Shenandoah Valley residents called "The Burning," destroying barns, mills, factories, and railroads throughout the Valley.

On October 19, 1864, Early surprised Sheridan's forces with a surprise attack at Cedar Creek. Sheridan, who heard artillery fire, raced the ten miles from Winchester to the battlefield to rally his men. Together with reinforcements from the Union 6th Corps, Sheridan secured a decisive victory and control of most of the Valley. At Appomattox Court House on April 9, 1865, Sheridan's cavalry blocked the continued retreat of the Army of Northern

Virginia and thus helped to secure an end to the war in Virginia.

## EDWIN M. STANTON
## UNION

Stanton, a lawyer and politician before the Civil War, was appointed secretary of war in 1862 and charged with restoring the reputation of a war department that had been accused of inefficiency and profiteering. He was effective in organizing the huge war department, but he and Lincoln often disagreed, particularly on cases of military discipline and pardon.

In the spring of 1862, Stanton tried to manage the Shenandoah Valley Campaign from Washington, and eventually diverted General Irvin McDowell from the operations against Richmond.

After the Second Battle of Manassas (Bull Run), Stanton denounced the failure by General George McClellan to reinforce General John Pope and charged McClellan with incompetence and insubordination. Other members of Lincoln's cabinet joined Stanton in the recommendation to remove McClellan from command. Lincoln refused, instead making McClellan head of the defenses of Washington, D.C.

Although the Lincoln-Stanton partnership was awkward at times, it was characterized by strong loyalty to one another and to the Union.

Portrait photos of Civil War Leaders and Generals are from the Library of Congress Prints and Photographs Division and the National Archives and Records Administration.

# Further Reading

## Leadership & Generalship

Davis, William C. 1999. *The Commanders of the Civil War.* Salamander Books.

Eicher, John H. and David J. Eicher. 2001. *Civil War High Commands.* Stanford University Press.

Foote, Shelby. 1958–1974. *The Civil War: A Narrative.* 3 volumes. Random House.

Gallagher, Gary W. 2011. *The Union War.* Harvard University Press.

Gallagher, Gary and Joseph T. Glatthaar. 2004. *Leaders of the Lost Cause: New Perspectives on the Confederate High Command.* Stackpole Books.

Glatthaar, Joseph T. 1994. *Partners in Command: The Relationship between Leaders in the Civil War.* The Free Press.

Goodwin, Doris Kearns. 2005. *Team of Rivals: The Political Genius of Abraham Lincoln.* Simon & Schuster.

Grimsley, Mark. 1995. *The Hard Hand of War: Union Military Policy Towards Southern Civilians, 1861–1865.* Cambridge University Press.

Hattaway, Herman and Archer Jones. 1983. *How the North Won: A Military History of the Civil War.* University of Illinois Press.

Krick, Robert K. 2002. *The Smoothbore Volley that Doomed the Confederacy.* Louisiana State University Press.

Nevins, Allan. 1947–1971. *Ordeal of the Union.* Charles Scribner's Sons.

Rable, George C. 1994. *Confederate Republic: A Revolution against Politics.* University of North Carolina Press.

Reardon, Carol. 2012. *With a Sword in One Hand and Jomini in the Other: The Problem of Military Thought in the Civil War North.* University of North Carolina Press.

Vandiver, Frank E. 1956. *Rebel Brass: The Confederate Command System.* Louisiana State University Press.

Warner, Ezra J. 1959. *Generals in Gray: Lives of the Confederate Commanders.* Louisiana State University Press.

Warner, Ezra J. 1964. *Generals in Blue: Lives of the Union Commanders.* Louisiana State University Press.

Wright, Marcus J. 1983. *General Officers of the Confederate Army.* J. M. Carroll & Co.

## Abraham Lincoln

Ballard, Colin R. 1952. *The Military Genius of Abraham Lincoln.* World Publishing Co. First published 1926.

Basler, Roy P., editor. 1953–1955. *The Collected Works of Abraham Lincoln.* 9 volumes. Rutgers University Press.

Boritt, Gabor S. 1994. *Lincoln and the Economics of the American Dream.* University of Illinois Press. First published 1978.

Burlingame, Michael. 2008. *Abraham Lincoln: A Life,* 2 volumes. Johns Hopkins University Press.

Burlingame, Michael. 2002. *Dispatches from Lincoln's White House: The Anonymous Civil War Journalism of Presidential Secretary William O. Stoddard.* University of Nebraska Press.

Catton, Bruce. 1951. *Mr. Lincoln's Army,* Doubleday.

Chadwick, Bruce. 1999. *The Two American Presidents: A Dual Biography of Abraham Lincoln and Jefferson Davis.* Birch Lane Press.

Foner, Eric. 2010. *The Fiery Trial: Abraham Lincoln and American Slavery.* W. W. Norton & Co.

McPherson, James M. 2008. *Tried by War: Abraham Lincoln as Commander in Chief.* Penguin.

Neely, Mark E., Jr. 1991. *The Fate of Liberty: Abraham Lincoln and Civil Liberties.* Oxford University Press.

Theater at Shiloh, Vicksburg, and Chickamauga. He also accompanied General Jubal Early in the 1864 Shenandoah Valley Campaign and the Raid on Washington.

In 1864, Breckinridge took command of and reorganized Confederate forces in southwestern Virginia, leading raids into northeastern Tennessee and achieving victory at Saltville, Virginia. In February of 1865, he was appointed Confederate secretary of war by Jefferson Davis. Though he had little time in that position, he favored a respectable surrender for the Confederacy rather than a futile and bloody continuance of fighting. During the evacuation of Richmond, he ensured that the Confederate archives were captured intact by Union forces, so that the Confederate side of the war was documented for history.

### BENJAMIN F. BUTLER
### UNION

Butler was a Massachusetts politician who served as a Union general during the Civil War. Though popular, Butler was frequently charged with corruption, abuse of power, and, as a political general, incompetence. Nevertheless, he made many contributions to the war effort, including the "contraband of war" decision that allowed the Union army to employ escaped slaves for work on fortifications. This helped prepare the way for emancipation.

During the war, Butler served as an administrator for occupied regions in Virginia and in New Orleans, Louisiana, where he was unpopular. In May of 1864, commanding the Army of the James,

Butler was to move against Richmond and Petersburg in conjunction with a southward movement by General Ulysses S. Grant. But rather than strike immediately at Petersburg, Butler's offensive bogged down east of Richmond at Bermuda Hundred.

Butler commanded the Army of the James through much of the campaign to capture Richmond, but his mismanagement of the January 1865, expedition against Fort Fisher, North Carolina, prompted Grant to remove him from command.

## JEFFERSON DAVIS
## CONFEDERATE

Before being elected president of the Confederate States of America, Davis was a veteran of the Mexican War, U.S. senator from Mississippi, and secretary of war under President Franklin Pierce. Davis was selected to serve as provisional president of the Confederacy in 1861, though he did not seek or appear to want the job. A war hero, slaveholder, and longtime advocate of states' rights, Davis was a moderate, and this strengthened his appeal in southern states, such as Virginia, that had not yet seceded in the spring of 1861.

Davis's reputation suffered during the war. He antagonized many in the Confederacy with his increasing willingness to favor centralized power over states' rights, imposing conscription, martial law, taxes, and regulations on the economy.

With regard to his military leadership, Davis is criticized for failing to manage his generals effectively. He established a close relationship with Robert E. Lee, but his relationships with other generals were not as good, and discord among them intensified over time. Davis's decision to relieve General Joseph E. Johnston, who was careful but capable, and replace him with General John Bell Hood, resulted in the loss of Atlanta and the eventual loss of an army.

Davis fled Richmond on April 3, 1865. Union cavalry captured him near Irwinville, Georgia, on May 10, 1865, and imprisoned him for two years at Fort Monroe, Virginia. He was indicted for treason in 1866 but was never tried.

## Jubal Early
### Confederate

Although Early opposed secession, when Virginia left the Union he accepted the colonelcy of the 24th Virginia Infantry and was promoted to brigadier general after the First Battle of Manassas (Bull Run).

Wounded at Williamsburg in 1862, Early returned two months later and served in most battles in the Eastern Theater. In 1864, he was promoted to lieutenant general and took command of the 2nd Corps.

As commander of the 2nd Corps, Early defeated the Union army under David Hunter in the Shenandoah Valley, and advanced into Maryland, menacing Washington, D.C. General Philip Sheridan, with Union reinforcements in the Valley, overpowered Early's forces in September 1864, at the Battle of Cedar Creek. After that, Early's command ceased to be an effective force to resist Federal control of the Valley.

## John B. Gordon
### Confederate

Without any prior military experience, Gordon served as colonel of the 6th Alabama Infantry in the Army of Northern Virginia. During the Battle of Antietam (Sharpsburg), he held the Sunken Road until five wounds rendered him unconscious. He recovered, returned to service, and was promoted to brigadier general.

During the 1864 Overland Campaign, Gordon proved to be an able commander and was promoted to major general. He led a division of General Jubal Early's army in the Shenandoah Valley Campaign, although he did not get along with Early. After the Confederate defeat at the Battle of Cedar Creek, Gordon led the 2nd Corps of the Army of Northern Virginia until the end of the war.

In March 1865, Gordon commanded an unsuccessful assault on Fort Stedman, near Petersburg, and participated in critical actions during Lee's retreat toward Appomattox. At Appomattox, he led his men in the last charge of the Army of Northern Virginia. On April 12, 1865, Gordon's troops officially surrendered.

## ULYSSES S. GRANT
## UNION

Grant began the Civil War as colonel of the 21st Illinois Infantry, and eventually rose to general-in-chief of all Union armies. Victories in the Western Theater at Fort Henry, Fort Donelson, Shiloh, and Vicksburg from 1862 through 1863 made Grant a nationally known figure, and in February 1864 Lincoln promoted Grant to lieutenant general. Grant arrived in Virginia in March 1864, taking the field with the Army of the Potomac instead of directing the war from an office in Washington, D.C.

Grant launched simultaneous offensives in all theaters of the war, keeping pressure on Confederate armies. In Virginia, Union forces engaged Lee's army at the Battle of the Wilderness and relentlessly pushed them toward Richmond. During a month of nearly constant combat, casualties mounted and amplified condemnation by Grant's critics. After nine months in front of Petersburg and Richmond, Grant broke Lee's lines on April 2, 1865, and ultimately trapped Lee at Appomattox Court House.

Grant accepted the surrender of the Army of Northern Vir-

Wert, Jeffry D. 2005. *The Sword of Lincoln: The Army of the Potomac.* Simon & Schuster.

Wilson, Douglas L. 1998. *Honor's Voice: The Transformation of Abraham Lincoln.* Knopf.

Wilson, Douglas L. and Rodney O. Davis. 1998. *Herndon's Informants: Letters, Interviews, and Statements about Abraham Lincoln.* University of Illinois Press.

## JEFFERSON DAVIS

Chadwick, Bruce. 1999. *The Two American Presidents: A Dual Biography of Abraham Lincoln and Jefferson Davis.* Birch Lane Press.

Cooper, William J. 2008. *Jefferson Davis and the Civil War Era.* Louisiana State University Press.

Cooper, William J. 2000. *Jefferson Davis, American.* Knopf.

Davis, William C. 1991. *Jefferson Davis: The Man and His Hour.* HarperCollins.

Escott, Paul D. 1978. *After Secession: Jefferson Davis and the Failure of Confederate Nationalism.* Louisiana State University Press.

Woodworth, Steven E. 1995. *Davis and Lee at War.* University Press of Kansas.

Woodworth, Stephen E. 1990. *Jefferson Davis and his Generals: The Failure of Confederate Command in the West.* University Press of Kansas.

## ULYSSES S. GRANT

Bonekemper, Edward H., III. 2004. *A Victor, Not a Butcher: Ulysses S. Grant's Overlooked Military Genius.* Regnery.

Bunting III, Josiah. 2004. *Ulysses S. Grant.* Times Books.

Catton, Bruce. 1954. *U. S. Grant and the American Military Tradition.* Little, Brown.

Fuller, J. F. C. 1957. *Grant and Lee, A Study in Personality and Generalship.* Indiana University Press.

Longacre, Edward G. 2006. *General Ulysses S. Grant: The Soldier And The Man.* De Capo Press.

McFeely, Mary Drake and William S. McFeely, editors. 1990. *Ulysses S. Grant: Memoirs and Selected Letters.* Library of America.

## ROBERT E. LEE

Dowdey, Clifford and Louis H. Manarin, editors. 1961. *The Wartime Papers of Robert E. Lee.* Little, Brown.

Freeman, Douglas Southall. 1957. *Lee's Dispatches: Unpublished Letters of General Robert E. Lee, CSA.* Putnam.

Freeman, Douglas Southall. 1942–1944. *Lee's Lieutenants: A Study in Command.* 3 volumes. Charles Scribner's Sons.

Freeman, Douglas Southall. 1934. *R. E. Lee: A Biography.* Charles Scribner's Sons.

Fuller, J. F. C. 1957. *Grant and Lee, A Study in Personality and Generalship.* Indiana University Press.

Gallagher, Gary W. 2004. *Lee and His Generals in War and Memory.* Louisiana State University Press.

Gallagher, Gary W. 2001. *Lee and His Army in Confederate History.* University of North Carolina Press.

Gallagher, Gary W., editor. 1996. *Lee the Soldier.* University of Nebraska Press.

Pryon, Elizabeth Brown. 2007. *Reading the Man: A Portrait of Robert E. Lee through his Private Letters.* Viking.

Robertson, James I., Jr. 2005. *Robert E. Lee: Virginian Soldier, American Citizen.* Athenaeum.

Wert, Jeffry D. 2011. *A Glorious Army: Robert E. Lee's Triumph, 1862–1863.* Simon & Schuster.

Woodworth, Steven E. 1995. *Davis and Lee at War.* University Press of Kansas.

## SHENANDOAH VALLEY CAMPAIGN 1862

Cozzens, Peter. 2008. *Shenandoah 1862: Stonewall Jackson's Valley Campaign.* University of North Carolina Press.

Ecelbarger, Gary. 2003. *Three Days in the Shenandoah: Stonewall Jackson at Front Royal and Winchester.* University of Oklahoma Press.

Gallagher, Gary W., editor. 2009. *The Shenandoah Valley Campaign of 1862*. University of North Carolina Press.

Krick, Robert K. 2002. *Conquering the Valley*. Louisiana State University Press.

Tanner, Robert G. 1976. *Stonewall in the Valley: Thomas J. "Stonewall" Jackson's Shenandoah Valley Campaign Spring 1862*. Doubleday.

## Shenandoah Valley Campaign 1864

Gallagher, Gary W., editor. 2006. *The Shenandoah Valley Campaign of 1864*. University of North Carolina Press.

Heatwole, John L. 1998. *The Burning: Sheridan in the Shenandoah Valley*. Rockbridge Publishing.

Knight, Charles R. 2010. *Valley Thunder: The Battle of New Market and the Opening of the Shenandoah Valley Campaign, May 1864*. Savas Beatie.

Mahr, Theodore C. 1992. *The Battle of Cedar Creek: Showdown in the Shenandoah October 1–30, 1864*. H. E. Howard.

Stackpole, Edward J. 1992. *Sheridan in the Shenandoah: Jubal Early's Nemesis*. Stackpole Books.

Wert, Jeffrey. 2010. *From Winchester to Cedar Creek: The Shenandoah Campaign of 1864*. Southern Illinois University Press.

## Other Civil War Leaders

Alexander, Edward Porter. 1998. *Fighting for the Confederacy: The Personal Recollections of General Edward Porter Alexander*. Edited by Gary W. Gallagher. University of North Carolina Press.

Cooling, Benjamin Franklin. 1989. *Jubal Early's Raid on Washington 1864*. Nautical & Aviation Publishing Company of America.

Cozzens, Peter and Robert I. Girardi, editors. 1998. *The Military Memoirs of General John Pope*. University of North Carolina Press.

Hollandsworth, James G. 1998. *Pretense of Glory: The Life of General Nathaniel P. Banks*. Louisiana State University Press.

Krick, Robert K. 1990. *Stonewall Jackson at Cedar Mountain*. University of North Carolina Press.

Lee, Susan P. 1991. *Memoirs of William Nelson Pendleton.* Sprinkle Publications.

Piston, William G. 1990. *Lee's Tarnished Lieutenant: James Longstreet and His Place in Southern History.* University of Georgia Press.

Reardon, Carol. 1997. *"I Have Been a Soldier All My Life": Gen. James Longstreet, CSA.* Farnsworth Military Impressions.

Robertson, James I., Jr. 1997. *Stonewall Jackson: The Man, the Soldier, the Legend.* MacMillan Publishing USA.

Sears, Stephen W. 1988. *George B. McClellan: The Young Napoleon.* Ticknor & Fields.

Thomas, Benjamin P. and Harold M. Hyman. 1980. *Stanton: The Life and Times of Lincoln's Secretary of War.* Greenwood Press.

Wert, Jeffry D. 2008. *Cavalryman of the Lost Cause: A Biography of J.E.B. Stuart.* Simon & Schuster.

Wert, Jeffry D. 1994. *General James Longstreet: The Confederacy's Most Controversial Soldier.* Simon & Schuster.

Wheelan, Joseph. 2012. *Terrible Swift Sword: The Life of General Philip H. Sheridan.* Da Capo Press.

Wittenberg, Eric J. 2002. *Little Phil: A Reassessment of the Civil War Leadership of Gen. Philip H. Sheridan.* Potomac Books.

Further Reading recommendations were contributed by Leadership and Generalship conference participants.

## Contributors

**JOHN W. KNAPP** is Superintendent Emeritus of the Virginia Military Institute and currently holds the Floyd D. Gottwald, Jr. '43 Visiting Professorship in Leadership and Ethics at the Institute. A 1954 graduate of VMI, he returned to serve on the faculty in 1959 after a period of active duty in the U.S. Army, earned masters and doctoral degrees from the Johns Hopkins University, and rose through the academic ranks at VMI until his appointment as superintendent in 1989. At that time he retired after a 35-year career in the U.S. Army Reserves with the rank of major general.

Since his retirement from VMI in 1995, he has been active in numerous civic and professional capacities, including 10 years of service on Lexington City Council, the last eight of which were as mayor of the city. In 2008, he was promoted to the rank of lieutenant general in the Virginia Militia.

**JOSIAH BUNTING III** is president of the Harry Frank Guggenheim Foundation in New York City. He is a graduate of the Virginia Military Institute and of the University of Oxford. He served as VMI superintendent from 1995 to 2002 and is now superintendent emeritus. His most recent book is a biography of Ulysses S. Grant, and he is completing a biography of George C. Marshall. Mr. Bunting lives with his family in Fauquier County, Virginia.

**WILLIAM J. COOPER** is a Boyd Professor at Louisiana State University. He received his bachelors degree from Princeton

University and his Ph.D. from Johns Hopkins University. He has been a Fellow of the Guggenheim Foundation and the National Endowment for the Humanities, and was a recipient of the *Los Angeles Times* Book Award for Biography. He is also a past president of the Southern Historical Association. His books include: *The South and the Politics of Slavery, 1828-1856*; *Liberty and Slavery: Southern Politics to 1860*; *Jefferson Davis, American*; and *Jefferson Davis and the Civil War Era*.

**PETER COZZENS** is a career foreign service officer and author of sixteen critically acclaimed books on the American Civil War and the Indian Wars of the American West. All of Cozzens' books have been selections of the Book of the Month Club, History Book Club, or the Military Book Club. Cozzens' *This Terrible Sound: The Battle of Chickamauga* and *The Shipwreck of Their Hopes: The Battles for Chattanooga* were both Main Selections of the History Book Club and were chosen by *Civil War Magazine* as two of the 100 greatest works ever written on the Civil War. His most recent book, *Shenandoah 1862: Stonewall Jackson's Valley Campaign*, received a *Choice Magazine* Outstanding Academic Title award in 2010. The Easton Press reprinted *This Terrible Sound* for inclusion in their Library of the Civil War collection.

**GARY W. GALLAGHER** is John L. Nau III Professor in the History of the American Civil War at the University of Virginia. A native of Los Angeles, California, he received his B.A. from Adams State College of Colorado and his M.A. and Ph.D. from the University of Texas at Austin. He taught for twelve years at Penn State University before joining the faculty of the University of Virginia in 1998.

He is author or editor of more than thirty books, including *The Confederate War*, *Lee and His Generals in War and Memory*, *The Myth of the Lost Cause and Civil War History* (co-edited with Alan T. Nolan), *Causes Won, Lost, and Forgotten: How Hollywood and Popular Art Shape What We Know About the Civil War*, and *The Union War*. He serves as editor of two book series for the University of North Carolina Press, has appeared regularly on the Arts and Entertainment Network's series Civil War Journal, and has participated in more than three dozen other television projects in the field.

Active in the field of historic preservation, Gallagher was president from 1987 to mid-1994 of the Association for the Preservation of Civil War Sites. He served as a member of the Board of the Civil War Trust and has given testimony about preservation before Congressional committees.

**ROBERT K. KRICK** grew up in Northern California. He has lived and worked on east coast battlefields for more than four decades. For thirty years he was Chief Historian of Fredericksburg & Spotsylvania National Military Park. Krick is author of twenty books and more than 200 articles. *Stonewall Jackson at Cedar Mountain* won three national awards, including the Douglas Southall Freeman Prize for Best Book in Southern History. *Conquering the Valley: Stonewall Jackson at Port Republic* was a main selection of the History Book Club and a selection of the Book of the Month Club. His latest book is *Civil War Weather in Virginia*. During 2003–2006, Krick worked under contract on the National Museum of the Marine Corps, writing most of the words on the walls of that new museum.

**MARK E. NEELY JR.** is McCabe-Greer Professor of the History of the Civil War Era and senior historian in residence at Pennsylvania State University. He is author or coauthor of eleven books, including *The Union Divided: Party Conflict in the Civil War North* and *The Union Image: Popular Prints of the Civil War North*. In 1992, he won the Pulitzer Prize for *The Fate of Liberty*, which also won the Bell I. Wiley Prize.

**CAROL REARDON** is George Winfree Professor of American History at Penn State University. An expert on the Civil War and Vietnam eras, she is the author of many books and articles about the U.S. military. Her titles include *Soldiers and Scholars: The U.S. Army and the Uses of Military History, 1865–1920*, *Pickett's Charge in History and Memory*, and *Launch the Intruders: A Naval Attack Squadron in the Vietnam War, 1972*. She was President of the Society for Military History, and is a member of the National Advisory

Board of the Civil War Trust.

**JAMES I. ROBERTSON, JR.**, an Alumni Distinguished Professor Emeritus at Virginia Tech, is one of the most distinguished names in Civil War history. A nationally acclaimed teacher and lecturer, he has written or edited two dozen books on the Civil War era. His biography of Stonewall Jackson won eight national awards and was the basis for the movie Gods and Generals. His most recent book is *The Untold Civil War: Exploring the Human Side of War*. Early in his career, Robertson was appointed executive director of the U.S. Civil War Centennial Commission by President John F. Kennedy. Today he serves on the Virginia Sesquicentennial of the American Civil War Commission, appointed by the Virginia General Assembly. Robertson lives on the Potomac River near the birthplaces of George Washington and Robert E. Lee.

**JEFFRY D. WERT**, a native of central Pennsylvania, is a historian, author, and lecturer of Civil War history. He graduated from the Lock Haven University, earned a M.A. in history from Penn State University, and taught at Penns Valley Area High School for 33 years, retiring in 2002. He has written nine books on the Civil War, two of which were awarded the Laney Prize: *A Brotherhood of Valor* and *The Sword of Lincoln*. Another book, Gettysburg, Day Three, was nominated for a Pulitzer Prize and a National Book Award. His newest work, *A Glorious Army*, has also been nominated for a National Book Award. He has also received the William Woods Hassler Award for contributions to Civil War studies. He has appeared on the television series Civil War Journal and other documentaries. He has written more than two hundred articles, columns, and essays for history journals and magazines and has lectured extensively throughout the country.

# Index

1st Corps (Confederate), 33–34, 101, 111
1st Maryland Infantry, 80
2nd Corps (Confederate), 87, 115, 116
2nd Massachusetts Infantry, 107
3rd South Carolina Infantry, 34
5th Corps (Union), 78
6th Alabama Infantry, 115
6th Corps (Union), 88, 90, 125
6th North Carolina Infantry, 33
7th South Carolina Cavalry, 37
9th Corps (Union Army), 73
15th New Jersey Infantry, 75
19th Corps (Union Army), 88, 90
21st Illinois Infantry, 56, 116
54th Massachusetts Infantry, 107
Adams, Charles Francis, 73–74
Alexander, Edward Porter, 31, 34, 35, 100–101, 111
Allan, William, 31
Allegheny Mountains, 80, 87, 94
American Revolutionary War, 18–19, 58
Antietam (Sharpsburg) (MD), 98, 102, 115, 120, 122–123
Appalachian Mountains, 63
Appomattox (VA), 27, 95, 100, 111, 116, 119, 120–122, 124–125
Argonne Forest (France), 60

Armstrong, Jack, 10
Army of Northern Virginia, 28, 37, 41, 43–44, 46, 48–50, 69, 81–83, 86, 98, 100–101, 106, 111, 115–116, 119, 121–125
Army of Tennessee, 25, 70, 119
Army of the James, 70, 113–114
Army of the Potomac, 66, 69, 75–77, 79, 81, 85, 91, 94, 103
Army of the Shenandoah, 78, 85, 90, 112, 117, 125
Army of the Tennessee, 119–120
Army of West Virginia, 90
Atlanta (GA), 24, 70, 91, 99, 105, 114, 119, 121
Aurora Borealis, 44–45
Ballard, Colin R., 12–13
Baltimore (MD), 87
Banks, Nathaniel, 70, 77–82, 112
Belmont (MO), 69
Bemiss, Samuel Merrifield, 36
Bennett, James Gordon, 64
Bennett, John Wheeler, 60–61
Berryville (VA), 91, 93
Black Hawk War, 5–6, 120
Bloody Angle, 98
Blue Ridge Mountains, 80–81, 94
Boritt, Gabor S., 9, 12–13
Boswell's Tavern, 34

Bragg, Braxton, 24–25, 69, 122
Brandy Station (VA), 63
Breckinridge, John C., 86, 112–113
Brown, Joseph, 22
Buckner, Simon Bolivar, 57
Buckner, Simon Bolivar, Jr., 57
Bull Run (Manassas) (VA), 8–9, 32, 98, 111, 115, 117, 118, 119, 122, 125, 126
Bulwer-Lytton, Edward, 56
Burns, Ken, 102
Burnside, Ambrose E., 33, 68, 73
Butler, Benjamin F., 70, 86, 113–114
Cass, Lewis, 5–6
Catton, Bruce, 99
Cedar Creek (VA), 85–86, 92, 94, 115–116, 125
Cedar Mountain (VA), 28, 112
Cemetery Hill, 31, 39
Chamberlain, Joshua L., 27
Chambersburg (PA), 87–88
Chancellorsville (VA), 28, 32–33, 39, 57, 99, 118, 120, 121
Charles Grier Sellers, 8
Charleston (SC), 22
Charlottesville (VA), 94
Chattanooga (TN), 59, 64, 69, 122
Chicago (IL), 91
Chickamauga (GA), 33, 113, 122
Churchill, Winston, 54
Clark, Mark W., 57
Clary, Royal, 5–6
Cold Harbor (VA), 56, 61, 68, 86
Columbus (KY), 23
Commander-in-chief, 1–13, 14, 16, 22, 25, 42, 66, 75
Congress, Confederate, 16–17, 20–21, 97
Congress, U.S., 4–5, 54, 69, 106–107, 112
Congressional Medal of Honor, 59
Connelly, Thomas, 34

Constitution, Confederate, 21
Constitution, U.S., 11
Contrabands, 111–112
Cooper, James Fenimore, 62
Crimean War, 15
Culp's Hill, 37
Culpeper (VA), 66, 76
Davis, Jefferson Finis, 15–25, 43–46, 48, 50, 60, 87, 97, 113, 114–115, 119
Deaton, Noah, 37
Democratic Party, 91, 123
Department of the Gulf, 112
Department of the Northwest, 125
Department of the Rappahannock, 78
Department of the Shenandoah, 78, 112
Department of the West, 119
desertion, 17, 21, 49–50
Doubleday, Abner, 100
Douglas, Henry Kyd, 29
Duke University, 33
Early, Jubal A., 87, 88, 90–95, 113, 115, 116, 117, 125
Eastern Theater, 63, 79, 111, 115
Eisenhower, Dwight, 53, 57
Election of 1864, 1, 45, 64, 85, 88, 90–91, 95, 105, 121, 123
Emancipation Proclamation, 6–7, 19, 106–107, 121
Ewell, Benjamin S., 82
Fairfax County (VA), 108
Federal oath, 27
Fisher's Hill (VA), 89–90, 93–94, 125
Fort Donelson (TN), 57, 69, 116
Fort Fisher (NC), 114
Fort Henry (TN), 69, 116
Fort Monroe (VA), 88, 115
Fort Sanders (TN), 33
Fort Stedman (VA), 116
Fort Sumter (SC), 120
Frederick the Great, 42

Fredericksburg (VA), 7, 33, 38, 78, 81, 118, 119
Freeman, Douglas Southall, 99–100
Fremont, John C., 77, 79, 81–83
Frobel, Anne S., 108
Front Royal (VA), 80, 82, 90
Fugitive Slave Law, 1
Galena (IL), 55, 66
Geary, John, 80–82
Georgetown (DC), 39
General-in-chief, 1, 8, 64, 67, 72, 78, 86, 91, 116, 121, 123, 125
Germ theory of disease, 7
Gettysburg (PA), 30–32, 57, 63, 67, 69, 88, 98–99, 102, 104, 108, 111, 120, 122, 123
Gordon, John B., 27, 115–116
Grant, Frederick D., 64, 66
Grant, Ulysses S., 10, 11, 50, 52, 53–62, 63–75, 86–92, 94, 98, 100, 101, 104, 112, 114, 116–117, 120, 121, 123, 125
Great Depression, 28
Greene, William, 6
guerrilla warfare, 7
Guild, Lafayette, 36
Halleck, Henry, 19, 78–79, 81
Halltown (WV), 90
Hanlon's Razor, 29, 39
Harpers Ferry (WV), 29, 84, 86–88, 94–95, 112
Harrisonburg (VA), 81, 82, 94
Haskell, Alexander Cheves, 37
Hay, John, 55
Hinson, William G., 37
Holliday, Frederick W. M., 28
Holly Springs (MS), 69
Holmes, Theophilis, 24
home front, 11, 20, 45, 98, 101, 104
Hood, John Bell, 100, 114
Hooker, Joseph, 64, 67–68
Hotchkiss, Jedediah, 31, 76, 79, 92

House of Representatives, U.S., 15
Housman, A.E., 54
Hunter, David, 86–87, 90, 115, 117
Inaugural Address of 1865, 97
Iron Brigade, 99
Jackson, Thomas J. "Stonewall," 29, 31, 32, 49, 56, 61, 62, 77–83, 88, 108, 112, 117–118
James River, 86, 101
Johnston, Albert Sidney, 24
Johnston, Joseph E., 23–24, 32, 34, 69, 81, 83, 100, 114, 118–119, 120
Jomini, Antoine Henri, 42–44, 48
Kernstown (VA), 76, 78, 87, 118
Kershaw, Joseph B., 91–92, 94
Knoxville (KY), 33, 111, 122
Lee, Fitzhugh, 91
Lee, George Washington Custis, 48
Lee, Robert E., 7, 26, 27–39, 40, 41–51, 55, 60, 61, 63, 68–71, 74, 86–91, 94, 95, 98, 99, 101, 106, 114, 116, 118, 119–120, 121, 122, 123, 124
Lexington (VA), 30–31, 86, 117, 123–124
Lincoln, Abraham, 1–13, 16, 19, 24, 54, 60, 64, 66, 67, 69, 71, 72, 74, 75, 77, 83, 85, 88, 89–91, 95, 97, 105–108, 112, 116, 118, 120–121, 122–123, 124, 126
Litwack, Leon F., 102–103
Logan, John, 56
Longstreet, James, 33–35, 49, 69, 101, 111, 121–122
Lost Cause, 28, 31, 37, 99
Lynchburg (VA), 70, 86–87, 117
MacArthur, Douglas, 53, 57
Mallory, Francis, 53
Manassas (Bull Run) (VA), 8–9, 32, 98, 111, 115, 117, 118, 119, 122, 125, 126
Manassas Gap Railroad, 82
Manassas Junction (VA), 78–79

## BOOKS FROM THE SERIES

### VOLUME ONE

*America on the Eve of the Civil War,* from the 2009 conference at the University of Richmond. Edited by Edward L. Ayers and Carolyn Martin, and published by UVA Press.

### VOLUME TWO

*Race, Slavery and the Civil War: The Tough Stuff of American History and Memory,* from the 2010 Signature Conference at Norfolk State University. Edited by James O. Horton and Amanda Kleintop, and published by the Virginia Sesquicentennial of the American Civil War Commission.

### VOLUME THREE

*Military Strategy in the American Civil War,* from the 2011 Signature Conference at Virginia Tech. Edited by James I. Robertson, Jr., and published by the Virginia Sesquicentennial of the American Civil War Commission.

### AVAILABLE ON DVD

*Virginia in the Civil War: A Sesquicentennial Remembrance,* an Emmy-nominated video documentary from Executive Producer James I. Robertson, Jr.

WWW.VIRGINIACIVILWAR.ORG/MARKETPLACE

ROCKHILL ELEMENTARY SCHOOL
50 WOOD DRIVE
STAFFORD, VIRGINIA 22556

DISCARD